BRITISH CARS AT LE MANS

AC □ ASTON MARTIN □ BENTLEY □ HEALEY
JAGUAR □ LOTUS □ MG □ TRIUMPH

DOMINIQUE PASCAL

A FOULIS Motoring Book

First published 1990

Published by:
Haynes Publishing Group
Sparkford, Nr Yeovil, Somerset
BA22 7JJ

Haynes Publications Inc.
861 Lawrence Drive, Newbury Park,
California 91320, USA

**British Library Cataloguing in
Publication Data**
British Cars at Le Mans
1. France. Le Mans. Racing cars.
Racing. Races = Grand Prix
d'endurance de Vingt-quatre heures
du Mans (Motor race), history
I. Title
ISBN 0-85429-872-X

Library of Congress catalog card number
90-83293

Editor: Robin Read
Translator: Sarah Darlington
Printed in England by: J.H. Haynes &
Co. Ltd

Author's Note

British Cars at Le Mans is the third in a series and follows *Porsche at Le Mans* and *Ferrari at Le Mans*, both published in French by EPA and in English by GT Foulis & Co Ltd. The first book, *Porsche at Le Mans*, covered the 426 Porsches raced at Le Mans between 1951 and 1983 and the second, *Ferrari at Le Mans*, covered the 262 cars raced at Le Mans by the Italian manufacturer between 1949 and 1984.

The number of British competitors in the Le Mans 24 Hours is so great that it has been necessary to be selective. This volume lists in their entirety the entrants from AC, Aston Martin (to which I have added Nimrod and Emka), Austin Healey and Healey, Bentley, Jaguar and Lister, Lotus, MG and Triumph. Presented here there are in total 326 cars, recorded chronologically and photographed in action at the greatest race in the world. Speeds and distances at Le Mans were recorded in kph and kilometres. For the English edition a conversion factor to mph/miles of 0.621 has been used.

D.P.

Contents

1923 page 5	1935 page 29	1957 page 64	1969 page 130
1924 page 6	1937 page 33	1958 page 68	1970 page 130
1925 page 7	1938 page 35	1959 page 74	1977 page 131
1926 page 8	1939 page 36	1960 page 80	1979 page 132
1927 page 9	1949 page 37	1961 page 86	1982 page 132
1928 page 11	1950 page 39	1962 page 94	1983 page 133
1929 page 14	1951 page 43	1963 page 115	1984 page 134
1930 page 18	1952 page 47	1964 page 120	1985 page 136
1931 page 20	1953 page 50	1965 page 124	1986 page 137
1932 page 22	1954 page 54	1966 page 125	1987 page 138
1933 page 24	1955 page 57	1967 page 126	1988 page 139
1934 page 26	1956 page 60	1968 page 127	1989 page 140

(Technical Summary page 143)   1990 page 141

Explanatory Note

Les Vingt-quatre Heures du Mans – known universally as 'Le Mans' plain and simple – is the greatest motor racing institution of them all.

The world's leading manufacturers, professional racing teams and drivers, with few exceptions, have all aspired to shine at – or perhaps even to win outright – the *Grand Prix d'Endurance* or its supporting categories. No race has had more influence on the design of high performance sporting cars than Le Mans; no event has produced so consistent a spectacle of international sporting competition than the grinding day-and-night drama conducted annually in a carnival atmosphere on the Sarthe circuit before countless thousands of spectators. The origins of the race may be traced to the imaginative vision of the doyen of French motor sport, Charles Faroux and his friend Georges Durand, who dreamed up an annual twenty-four hour event for catalogued sports-touring cars to begin in 1923, when the sports car concept itself was barely a decade old. Émile Coquille, French importer of the Rudge Whitworth centre-lock splined-hub wheel which in itself transformed motor-racing, put up 100,000 francs to finance the event, and the first great Trophy was the Rudge Whitworth Triennial Cup, to be awarded in 1925.

As the race became a regular annual event, the Triennial Cup was superseded by a series of Biennial Cups and from 1928 an 'official' outright winner of the Grand Prix d'Endurance was announced; parallel in importance to the Rudge Whitworth Biennial Cup competition.

In 1926, the entry competed for the first time for the Index of Performance award. This involves the use of an ingenious little formula to relate distance covered against a target by engine capacity, and became a category much beloved of students of the rule-book. Occasionally however, one had the impression that it was won (e.g. Aston Martin in 1950) by an unwitting outsider . . .

In 1959 the Index of Performance was supplemented by the fiendishly complex Index of Thermal Efficiency, this after a couple of years when the former (traditionally regarded as the preserve of French small-capacity entries) had been snatched by British and Italian competition. Immediately, the French regained their self-confidence and both trophies.

As the years rolled by, the regulations changed subtly to move away from insistence on 'same as you can buy' entries to admit a variety of more exotic alternatives including, in immediately pre- and post-war years, thinly-disguised Grand Prix cars and 'prototypes' of wildly expensive and exciting specification. From Bentley, Bugatti, Aston Martin, Alfa Romeo and MG sports cars in the pre-war years developed the purpose-built Ferrari, Lago Talbot, Jaguar and later Aston Martin entries of 1949 and beyond. In 1952 Mercedes-Benz returned to the fray, and won in celebration of the *Wirtschaftswunder*. During the Sixties the giant Ford Motor Company financed the manufacture and operation of a team of special cars for the express purpose of seizing the priceless seal of Le Mans success to mark by association their mundane production cars as performance-orientated . . . Meanwhile Porsche painstakingly pursued the triumph of development over design to build up an apparently unassailable position of superiority at the Sarthe. And then Jaguar and Mercedes tried again. While the giants of the *Vingt-quatre Heures* dominated the scene, a host of minor players were to be observed snapping at their heels. The British – always regarding Le Mans as half at least their own – were particularly assiduous in their endeavours, with minor manufacturers and the less glamorous – MG, Triumph, Austin Healey and others – frequently striving for success in the smaller capacity classes and Indices.

This magnificent race, born in a region of unrivalled significance in the history of motor sport (it was also the scene of the first French GP in 1906) has been run over a little-changed (two minor contractions in 1929 and 1932 and a few FIA-inspired chicanes on the Mulsanne Straight from 1990) circuit since inception. There have been minor interruptions and threats (the French civil unrest of 1936, the Second World War and the reforming zeal of M. Balestre) but these have not detracted from the importance and character of the Greatest Race in the World.

R.R.

1923

This first Grand Prix d'Endurance was held on 26-27 May. It was raining and of the 35 cars entered, 33 arrived at the start line. Of these, the only British competitor finished an honourable fourth behind two Chenard & Walckers and a Bignan. For the record, the winner completed 1372.65 miles at an average speed of 57.21mph.

Bentley, No.8. Driven by Duff/Clement. This car finished fourth, having completed 112 laps and travelled a distance of 1201.32 miles in 24 hours at an average speed of 50.16mph. Officially under the regulations governing competition for the Rudge-Whitworth Triennial Cup no placings were made in terms of distance travelled. Competitors were required to maintain a minimum average speed to avoid disqualification which could take effect after the 12-hour mark in cases where the car had failed by 20% to average the set minimum. This Bentley was the only British car entered in the new race and was to be the first of a long series. It was thanks to John Duff that the love affair between Great Britain and Le Mans began on that very rainy weekend in May 1923. The Bentley set the lap record at 9m.39sec (66.70mph) in the 24th hour after a punctured fuel tank had slowed its progress. However, the future held for Bentley the consolation of five outright victories.

5

1924

In an attempt to avoid the rain, the race was scheduled for 14–15 June. There were six more starters than in the previous year's race, but again only one English entry. This year, Bentley's hopes were not to be dashed: the car was going to settle a score with no less than sixteen French marques who had all come to win.

Bentley, No.8. Driven by Duff/Clement. The car was placed first on distance (unofficially) having covered 1290.80 miles in 24 hours at an average speed of 53.78mph.

But for bad luck, this Bentley would have won the previous year. By its return to the Sarthe circuit, the Bentley dismayed the entire French motor industry which had come to Le Mans intent on a second victory. There was one hiccough during the Bentley's fine performance according to contemporary reports – the driver dropped the ignition key into the car's entrails and spent twenty minutes trying to find it!

1925

There were forty cars at the start of the third Le Mans race, which took place on 20–21 June. The 24 Hours was becoming a truly international contest with a greater number of foreign manufacturers including Diatto, OM, Sunbeam, Austin and Chrysler.

A Lorraine won at an average speed of 57.848mph over a total distance of 1388.13 miles.

Bentley, No.10, Driven by Kensington-Moir/Benjafield. This car retired after 203.80 miles.

The retirement of this car was the fault of Kensington-Moir; the car ran out of petrol before the authorised refuelling time.

Bentley, No.9. Driven by J. Duff/F. Clement. This car retired during the 64th lap, having travelled 686.47 miles.

Encouraged by the previous year's success, two Bentleys had come to the Le Mans circuit. Unfortunately no two years are alike. The float of one of the SU carburettors fitted to Bentley No.9 punctured causing petrol to pour out under the bonnet and catch fire.

1926

For the second consecutive year, a Lorraine took the laurels in the Le Mans 24 Hours. Moreover, the 100km/h barrier was truly broken. The Lorraine created a race record by achieving 106.35km/h (66.08mph) and completed a total of 1585 miles. None of the British cars was placed.

Bentley, No.9. Driven by Thistlethwayte/Gallop. This car retired on the 105th lap (broken valve) having completed 1126.24 miles.

Bentley, No.7. Driven by Davis/Benjafield. By the 23rd hour, Bentley No.7 was within five laps of the leader (the Lorraine of Bloch/Rossignol) when it skidded on the Mulsanne Corner and smashed into the barrier. It was unable to finish the race and retired. The minimum distance set was 1284.68 miles and this was reached by the 21st hour. The car retired on the 138th lap having completed 1480.20 miles when disaster struck.

Bentley, No.8. Driven by Duller/Clement. This car retired after 72 laps and 772.28 miles. As with No.9, valve problems conspired to bring the car to a halt. The engine specification of these Bentleys was a capacity of 2997cc with a bore and stroke of 80 x 149mm; twin SU carburettors were fitted. Drum brakes were fitted to all four 820 x 120 wheels.

1927

Bentley was victorious once again, this time against rather reduced opposition. The supremacy of the Bentleys was seriously contested only by Laly and Chassagne in The Ariès which had to retire two hours from the finish. The Bentley Boys had become part of the Le Mans legend.

Bentley, No.1. Driven by Clement/Callingham. In spite of its 4½-litre engine and a record lap in 8min 46sec, this Bentley, the widely-tipped favourite, was forced to retire on the 35th lap after the White House disaster.

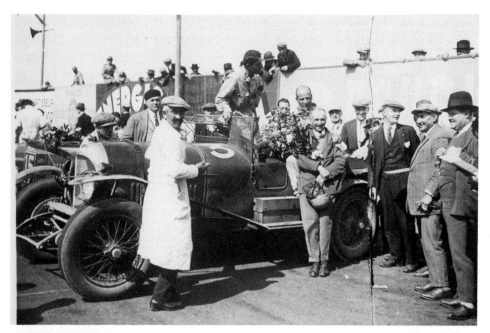

Bentley, No.3. Driven by Benjafield/Davis. This car was placed (still unofficially) first on distance after completing 1471.65 miles in 24 hours, at an average speed of 61.32mph. Bentley No.3, the drivers more fortunate than in 1926, was the only Bentley to be placed and won the 3-litre category as well as the overall race. A miraculous survivor of the White House débâcle, the car was returned to the pits by 'Sammy' Davis with a twisted chassis. The car was patched up and continued its battle with the Ariès which went on to retire towards 2.30pm. This left the field open to the old 3-litres to redeem the honour of the Bentley Boys.

Bentley, No.2. Driven by d'Erlanger/Duller. This 3-litre Bentley was also involved in the White House crash and retired on the 34th lap.

The three Bentleys, not quite in numerical order and with hoods up, making their way to the start.

1928

In 1928 there was again only a small number of competitors – thirty-three cars at the start compared with twenty-two the previous year. There were plenty of foreign cars, however, and a new British marque – Aston Martin – made its first appearance at Le Mans. Aston Martin was not to achieve a victory in the Le Mans 24 Hours for another 31 years.

Bentley, No.2. Driven by Clement/Benjafield. This 4½-litre Bentley, which was placed third at the half-way point, had completed more than 760 miles when it retired during the 71st lap. The car retired due to a fractured oil pipe and/or a burst water hose.

Bentley, No.3. Driven by Birkin/Chassagne. The car was placed fifth (officially at last) on distance after completing 1451.12 miles in 24 hours, at an average speed of 60.46mph.
After a superb race and despite losing three hours with a puncture and collapsed wheel on the 20th lap, this Bentley qualified for 1929's race and the Biennial Cup. 'Tim' Birkin established a new lap record of 8min 7sec at an average speed of 79.29mph.

Bentley, No.4. Driven by Barnato/Rubin. This car was placed first on distance having completed 1658.61 miles in 24 hours, at an average speed of 69.11mph.

With Woolf Barnato at the wheel, the Bentley crossed the finishing line to win the new *Coupe Annuelle à la Distance* after an exciting duel with the Stutz during which both cars beat the lap record.

Barnato's new lap record of 8min 17sec was quickly superseded by Birkin in Bentley No.3. Bentley No.4's average speed was 77.69mph.

Aston Martin, No.25. Driven by Bertelli/Eyston. Capt. George Eyston, famous for his attempts at the land speed record, retired during the 32nd lap with a broken rear axle. These unusual, low-slung racing cars, designed by the talented Bertelli, were fitted with 64bhp engines and a four-speed gearbox.

Aston Martin, No.26. Driven by Bezzant/Paul. This Aston retired during the 82nd lap with a broken gear lever. It had completed 879.54 miles.

1929

1929 saw a fourth Le Mans victory for Bentley. In addition to this triumph, the first four places were taken by the familiar green cars. The Americans had also started to take an interest in Le Mans but the victor's crown was not yet to be theirs. French honour was redeemed only by two little Tractas, at the bottom of the classification.

Bentley, No.1. Entered by W.O. Bentley and driven by Barnato/Birkin. This car was placed first in distance having completed 1767.07 miles in 24 hours at an average speed of 73.63mph.

Bentley No.1 left in the lead and at the end of the first lap had outstripped the other Bentleys, Nos.8, 9, 10 and 11, in that order. This was the only Bentley fitted with the dual ignition 6½-litre engine. It also won the Biennial Cup, beating Benjafield and d'Erlanger's Bentley No.10.

Bentley had now won four Le Mans 24 Hour races – but there was much more to come.

Bentley, No.9. Entered by W.O. Bentley and driven by Dunfee/Kidston. This Bentley was placed second on distance having completed 1695.96 miles in 24 hours at an average speed of 70.68mph.

The Bentleys had become great favourites after their victory the previous year. This one, driven confidently and without fuss, finished barely 100km behind the winner, to win the 3–5-litre class.

Bentley, No.10. Entered by W.O. Bentley and driven by Benjafield/d'Erlanger. This car was placed third on distance after completing 1614.55 miles in 24 hours at an average speed of 67.27mph.

Once again, the Bentleys ran like clockwork throughout a superb race. Bentley's policy was to use British-made parts, and the cars were fitted with Delco ignition, Lucas dynamos and headlamps, Hartford shock absorbers (one of them, however, and it is not clear which, had Repusseau shock absorbers), Shell oil and Champion spark plugs. Charles Faroux – a Frenchman, of course – expressed the view that the Bentleys would not have had so many problems with their headlamps during the night if Marchal units had been fitted.

Bentley, No.8. Entered by W.O. Bentley and driven by Clement/Chassagne. This Bentley was placed fourth on distance after completing 1593.73 miles in 24 hours at an average speed of 66.41mph.

In contrast to the other Bentleys, Bentley No.8 was fitted with an ML magneto and KLG spark plugs. It is interesting that contemporary sources remark on the high standard of organisation of the Bentley pits and put them forward as a model of their type.

Bentley, No.11. Entered by W.O. Bentley and driven by Rubin/Earl Howe. This car retired with a broken magneto driveshaft during the seventh lap after completing only 71.16 miles. This was the first retirement of the race.

Like its stablemates, this four-cylinder Bentley had a maximum speed of ca. 100mph but was the only Bentley fitted with Perrot brakes.

1930

1930 saw Bentley's last victory at Le Mans. Bentley, together with La Lorraine, had demonstrated that isolated victories at Le Mans were to be the exception rather than the rule. With only seventeen participants, the 1930 race was the most poorly attended in the history of the Le Mans 24 Hours. Mercedes, Talbot and Bugatti however, all made an appearance and MG was seen at Le Mans for the first time.

Bentley Speed Six, No.3. Entered by W.O. Bentley and driven by Davis/Dunfee. 'Sammy' Davis, the journalist who worked for *The Autocar*, was driving when a piece of grit got in his eye and he had to be replaced by Dunfee. This did not last long, however; on the 21st lap Dunfee left the road on the Pont-lieue bend, ran aground in the sand, bent the front axle and was forced to retire.

Bentley, No.8. Entered by Miss Dorothy Paget, driven by Benjafield/Ramponi. Retired in the 21st hour during the 144th lap. In the early afternoon, piston trouble finished the race for this 'Blower' Bentley as it thundered past Les Hunaudières. By now the Bentleys were equipped with Bosch magnetos.

Bentley, No.9. Entered by Dorothy Paget, driven by Birkin/Chassagne. Retired on the 138th lap. Birkin, surprised by the lightning departure of the Mercedes, set off after it in hot pursuit. As a result, Bentley No.9 completed the fourth lap in a staggering 6min 48sec at a speed of 89.70mph to create a new lap record which was not bettered during the course of the race. Unfortunately, as a result of this skirmish, Birkin had to have the tyres changed and it is possible also that the engine suffered, because early in the afternoon, a con-rod failure forced retirement during the 21st hour.

Bentley Speed Six, No.2. Entered by W.O. Bentley and driven by Clement/Watney. Bentley No.2 was placed second on distance after completing 1760.02 miles in 24 hours at an average speed of 73.73mph. This last-minute team – Clement had in fact been due to drive Bentley No.7 which was withdrawn – drove a fine race. It is worth noting here that the 'blown' four-cylinder cars were actually faster than the six-cylinder Bentleys. If the thick night fog had not reduced its average speed, the winning Bentley might well have exceeded 3000km (1864.11 miles) during the 24 hours.

MG Midget, No.28. Entered by Huskinson and Fane and driven by Murton-Neale/Hicks. This car retired during the 82nd lap. The two MGs had the smallest engines in the race (only 847cc) and it was MG's first visit to Le Mans, although in latter years the little MGs were to become a familiar sight there. Sources differ on the cause of MG No.28's retirement as to whether it was a broken crankshaft or transmission failure that caused the problem.

Bentley Speed Six, No.4. Entered by W.O. Bentley and driven by Barnato/Kidston placed first on distance after completing 1821.03 miles in 24 hours at an average speed of 75.88mph. This was the fifth and last victory for Bentley at Le Mans and Woolf Barnato's third personal victory there. In fact, as Barnato had driven only three times at Le Mans, he had a 100 per cent success rate. With Birkin out, Barnato continued the struggle against Caracciola's Mercedes for ten hours.

With such a wealth of experience at Le Mans behind them, it is hardly surprising that the Bentleys had come properly prepared. The cars had duplicated electrical wiring, dual brake lights mounted on rubber, four hydraulic shock absorbers on each axle, and armoured HT leads.

Bentley No.4, which had also won the Le Mans 24 Hours in 1929, was converted into a single-seater and won the 500 Mile race at Brooklands in 1931 at a speed of 117mph.

MG Midget, No.29. Entered by Francis Samuelson and driven by him and Kindell. This MG was forced to retire during the 28th lap after five hours due to magneto problems although an alternative source suggests an oil pipe was at fault. The Midget's 30bhp engine was of 847cc with a bore and stroke of 57x83mm. An SU carburettor and three-speed gearbox were fitted. The wheels were fitted with Dunlop 4.00x19 tyres.

19

1931

For several years, the winds of fortune were to blow on Le Mans from the South – Alfa Romeo (albeit with English drivers) won the race in 1931 with a distance total of 1875 miles (more than 3000km) at an average speed of 77.90mph. Only 26 cars competed in the race, partly as a result of the economic depression which now gripped Europe.

Aston Martin, No.24. Entered by Aston Martin and driven by Cook/Bezzant. This car retired during the 111th lap after completing 1127 miles. Engine 1495cc, 69.3x99.06mm, SU carburettors, Dunlop tyres.

Aston Martin, No.25. Entered by Aston Martin and driven by Bertelli/Harvey. This Aston was placed fifth on distance after completing 1420.70 miles in 24 hours at an average speed of 59.20mph and won the 1500cc class.

Bentley, No.7. Entered by S. Bevan and driven by A. Bevan/Couper. This Bentley retired after 295 miles on the 29th lap with ignition problems.

MG Midget, No.31. Driven by Samuelson/Kindell. Despite an average speed of almost 53mph this Midget was not classified because it completed its last lap in 31min 28sec instead of the permitted 30min.

MG Midget, No.32. Entered by the Hon. Mrs Chetwynd and driven by Mrs Chetwynd/Mrs Stisted. The ladies retired this MG during the 30th lap with ignition failure.

Aston Martin, No.26. Entered by Aston Martin and driven by Newsome/Peacock. This Aston retired in the 126th lap after 1270 miles.

1932

Twenty-six competitors took part in the tough 1932 race following a new course which had been opened that year. The race was again won by an Alfa, driven this time by Sommer/Chinetti who completed 1835.55 miles in 24 hours at an average speed of 76.48mph. Two Astons, however, saved the honour of Great Britain.

Bentley, No.5. Entered by Trévoux and driven by Trévoux/'Mary' (Pierre Brousselet). This car retired in the first lap after an accident near the White House. Fortunately, Trévoux was wearing a helmet and escaped with facial bruising and a fractured wrist. Minoïa, in an Alfa Romeo, crashed into the overturned wreckage and also had to retire.

Aston Martin, No.21. Chassis No LM5. Entered by Aston Martin and driven by Bertelli/Driscoll. This Aston was placed seventh on distance, second in the 1½-litre class and secured the Rudge Whitworth Cup after completing 1409.32 miles in 24 hours at an average speed of 58.09mph.

Aston Martin, No.20. Entered by Aston Martin and driven by Newsome/Widengren. This car came fifth on distance after completing 1459.502 miles in 24 hours at an average speed of 60.81mph and won the 1100–1500cc class.

MG Midget, No.32. Entered by Samuelson and driven by Samuelson/Black. This MG – the baby of the race with an engine of only 747cc – was leading the Index of Performance when a punctured fuel tank forced it to retire on the 53rd lap. It had completed 478 miles.

Aston Martin, No.22. Entered by Aston Martin and driven by Peacock/Bezzant. Like the other two Aston Martins, No.22 had spark plug problems at the beginning of the race and was retired after 445 miles on the 53rd lap.

1933

1933 saw a third victory for Alfa Romeo and the prestigious crew Sommer/Nuvolari who completed 1953.61 miles at an average speed of 81.40mph. In addition to this success, Alfa Romeos took second and third. The 29 competitors included one American car, seven Italian, eleven French and ten British cars.

Aston Martin, No.24. Entered by Aston Martin and driven by Bertelli/Davis. This Aston was placed seventh on distance after completing 1461.62 miles in 24 hours at an average speed of 60.90mph.

Aston Martin, No.25. Entered by Aston Martin and driven by Driscoll/Penn-Hughes. This car was placed fifth on distance after completing 1583.37 miles in 24 hours at an average speed of 65.99mph. In addition, it won the 1500cc class and was placed second in the Biennial Cup behind Sommer/Nuvolari in the Alfa.

Aston Martin, No.26. Entered by Aston Martin and driven by Morris-Goodall/Mrs Wisdom. This Aston retired in the 84th lap with engine problems after completing 704.01 miles. 'Bill' Wisdom who was driving, had to return to the pits on foot.

Bentley, No.5. Driven by Gas/Trévoux and retired after 209 miles on the 25th lap. Louis Gas was driving when a violent skid resulted in a bent axle.

MG Midget, No.38. Entered by Black and driven by Black/Gibson. This Midget had to retire with a punctured radiator during the 125th lap after completing 1048 miles.

MG Midget, No.41. Entered by John Ludovic Ford and driven by Ford/Baumer. This MG was placed sixth on distance after completing 1482.15 miles in 24 hours at an average speed of 61.70mph. It won the 750cc class at an average of almost 100km/h (62mph)! The crew also did well in the Index of Performance (2nd).

1934

There were 44 cars at the start of this the twelfth Le Mans 24 Hour Race including a record British entry of nine cars. These were entirely Aston Martins and MGs; farewell the Bentley Boys. Alfa won the race for the fourth consecutive year with Chinetti/Étancelin finishing at a comparatively low average speed of 74.74mph. The distance covered was 1793.86 miles.

Aston Martin, No.20. Entered by A. Vincent. Driven by Tongue/Falkner. This car was placed tenth on distance having completed 1579.11 miles in 24 hours at an average speed of 65.80mph.

Aston Martin, No.21. Entered by Aston Martin and driven by Bertelli/Penn-Hughes. This car retired during the 59th lap after completing 494.63 miles. The race got off to a bad start for Bertelli, whose car went into a spin during the first lap. He continued the race but had lost time and was disqualified under Article 13 of the rules for not completing the minimum mileage in twelve hours.

Aston Martin, No.24. Entered by John Cecil Noel and driven by Noel/Wheeler. This car was placed eleventh on distance after completing 1513.37 miles in 24 hours at an average speed of 63.06mph.

Aston Martin, No.23. Entered by Aston Martin, driven by Morris-Goodall/Elwes and retired during the 155th lap after completing 1299.45 miles. The car was in second place before its retirement in the nineteenth hour.

Aston Martin, No.22. Entered by Aston Martin and driven by Fotheringham/Appleton. A sheared magneto drive key was responsible for the car's retirement during the 142nd lap after 1187.36 miles.

MG Magnette K3, No.34. Entered by Roy Eccles and driven by Martin/Eccles.
This MG Magnette was placed fourth on distance after completing 1655.97 miles in 24 hours at an average speed of 69.00mph. It also won the 1100cc class and came fourth in the special competition for cars using blended fuel (petrol/alcohol/benzole) sponsored by the Office Nationale des Combustibles Liquides (National Fuel Bureau).

MG Magnette K3, No.33. Entered by John Ludovic Ford and driven by Ford/Baumer. Retired during the 85th lap after 712.60 miles. This supercharged 1100cc MG gave a superb performance taking second place overall during the night before retiring with a punctured fuel tank during the tenth hour.

MG Midget, No.53. Entered by P. Maillard-Brune, and driven by Maillard-Brune/Druck. Retired during the 30th lap after completing approximately 251 miles having run a big end. (The car is on the right of the photograph.)

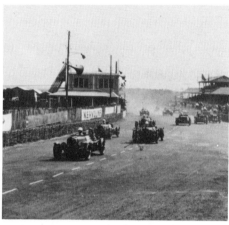

MG Midget, No.52. Entered by Madame Itier and driven by Mme Itier/Duruy. This Midget came seventeenth on distance after completing 1361.55 miles in 24 hours at an average speed of 56.73 and was second in the 1000cc class.

1935

The 1935 race, a British victory, was won by a Lagonda driven by Hindmarsh and Fontes. The car created a new Le Mans record by completing 1868.83 miles at an average speed of 77.85mph. There was also a record entry of 58 cars of which seven were MGs and seven Aston Martins.

Aston Martin Ulster, No.28. Entered by A. Vincent and driven by Penn-Hughes/Fotheringham. This Ulster left the course during the 45th lap and retired after completing only a little over 370 miles.

Aston Martin Ulster, No.27. Entered by J.C. Noel and driven by Elwes/Morris-Goodall. This car was placed twelfth on distance after completing 1649.95 miles in 24 hours at an average speed of 68.75mph.

Aston Martin Ulster, No.29. Entered by Roy Eccles and driven by Martin/Brackenbury This car came third on distance after completing 1805.44 miles in 24 hours at an average speed of 75.23mph. In addition to winning the 1500cc class and the Index of Performance Aston No.29 was constantly involved in the struggle for first place and despite its small capacity engine achieved 105mph on the Mulsanne Straight, which won the admiration of spectators and journalists alike.

Aston Martin Ulster, No.30. Entered by R. Percy Gardner and driven by Gardner/Beloë. This Ulster was placed fifteenth on distance after completing 1599.57 miles in 24 hours, at an average speed of 66.65mph.

Aston Martin Ulster, No.31. Entered by P.L. Donkin and driven by Donkin/Lord Hamilton. This car was placed eleventh on distance after completing 1670.18 miles in 24 hours at an average speed of 69.56mph.

Aston Martin Ulster, No.32. Entered by C.T. Thomas and driven by Thomas/Kenyon. This car was placed tenth after completing 1674.41 miles in 24 hours at an average speed of 69.77mph.

Aston Martin Ulster, No.33. Entered by F.L. Falkner and driven by Falkner/Clarke. This car was placed eighth on distance after completing 1701.02 miles in 24 hours, at an average speed of 70.88mph. This was a superb 'team' effort by the Aston Martins which finished very close together. (Aston Martin Ulster No.33 is shown in the photograph behind Singer No.48.)

MG K3 Magnette, No.39. Entered by Maurice H. Baumer and driven by Baumer/Ford. This MG retired with a broken piston on the 99th lap after completing 829.97 miles.

MG K3 Magnette, No.41. Entered by E. Hertzberger and driven by Hertzberger/Raph. This Franco-Dutch team was forced to retired on the 92nd lap after 771 miles with supercharger trouble.

MG K3 Magnette, No.42. Entered by F. Maillard-Brune and driven by Maillard-Brune/Druck. This car was placed ninth on distance after completing 1699.03 miles in 24 hours at an average speed of 70.86mph. This was a fine performance by the French team whose little MG won the 751–1100cc class in great style. The Singer which was second to the MG in this class came only sixteenth overall.

MG Midget, No.56. Entered by Capt. George Eyston and driven by Miss Joan Richmond/Mrs Simpson (Doreen Evans stands right). This Midget was placed 24th on distance after completing 1291.04 miles in 24 hours at an average speed of 53.79mph.

MG Midget, No.55. Entered by George Eyston and driven by Miss Doreen Evans/Miss Barbara Skinner. This car was placed 25th on distance after completing 1285.23 miles in 24 hours at an average speed of 53.55mph.

MG Midget, No.57. Entered by George Eyston and driven by Miss Margaret Allan/Mrs Colleen Eaton. This car was placed 26th on distance after completing 1276.82 miles in 24 hours at an average speed of 53.20mph.

MG Midget, No.58. Entered by P. Maillard-Brune and driven by Viale/Debille. This Midget retired during the 98th lap with super-charger problems after completing 821.59 miles.

1936

13 and 14 June 1936 were initially set aside for the 14th Le Mans 24 Hour race but the notorious strikes of that year led to its postponement.

At first it was hoped to put back the date to 20 – 21 June – Article 57 of the regulations preventing the date from being brought forward. The RAC, however, had already organized a race for the 20th so that date, too, proved unsuitable. Finally it seemed that the race would go ahead on 1 and 2 August.

Even as early as December 1935 the ACO (Automobile Club de l'Ouest) had received 47 entries for the following year's race. This included four Works Aston Martins (one for Fairchild/Brackenbury, one for Haardlem/Worst, a third for Benjafield and fourth for Elwes), two private Astons (Noel and Thomas), a Bentley (Hall), as well as two MGs (Eyston and Hertzberger).

On 23rd June, however, it was announced officially that the 1936 Le Mans 24 Hours had been cancelled.
1937

1937

1937 saw the resounding official return of Bugatti as Wimille/Benoist carried away the laurels with an average speed of 85.13mph and a distance of 2043.03 miles leading two Delahayes and a Delage. France had re-established her supremacy. Of forty-eight starters, the British contingent was made up of HRG, Aston Martin, MG, Singer, Austin, Frazer Nash, Lagonda and Riley.

Aston Martin Ulster, No.31. Driven by Morris-Goodall/Hitchens. The car came eleventh on distance, having covered 1624.19 miles in 24 hours at an average speed of 67.67mph and secured the Biennial Cup for 1935/1937.

MG Midget, No.54. Driven by Miss Stanley Turner/Miss Riddell. This car was placed sixteenth on distance after completing 1294.08 miles in 24 hours at an average speed of 53.92mph. These two young ladies were placed second-to-last in front of the little Simca 5, the Tail-end Charlie in the 1937 24 Hours.

Aston Martin Ulster, No.37. Driven by Skeffington/Murton-Neale. This car was placed fifth on distance after completing 1720.38 miles in 24 hours, at an average speed of 71.68mph. In addition to this superb fifth place, won in the face of more powerful competition, No.37 won the 1101 – 1500cc class and was third in the Index of Performance.

Aston Martin Ulster, No.32. Driven by Hertzberger/Debille and retired during the 136th lap after completing 1140.16 miles. With its 2-litre engine, this Aston, brilliantly driven by Hertzberger, more or less led its category for sixteen hours at an average speed of 74.56mph. It retired during the morning with a fractured oil pipe.

1938

1938 saw another French victory, this time for a Delahaye, driven by Chaboud/Trémoulet and completing 1976.53 miles at an average speed of 82.36mph. It was Delahaye's only victory in the Le Mans 24 Hour Race. The number of British competitors had dropped; there were only nine British cars including one Aston and two MGs.

Aston Martin Ulster, No.27. Driven by Hitchens/Morris-Goodall. A broken valve forced these veterans of the Le Mans 24 Hours to retire after 21 hours of a superb race. They had completed 150 laps and 1257.53 miles.

The skill of the mechanics had already been severely tested since they had changed a piston towards noon and the car had set off again to the cheers of the crowd to complete, unfortunately, only a few more laps.

MG, No.49. Driven by Bonneau/Mme Itier. This MG was placed twelfth on distance after completing 1384.13 miles in 24 hours at an average speed of 57.67mph. It stopped fourteen times in the pits which resulted in the car being stationary for 47min 30sec which in turn reduced the overall average speed to 60.89mph.

Madame Itier, the only woman to be placed overall, also came fourth in the 751 – 1100cc category behind a Singer and two Simcas and the MG was placed tenth in the Index of Performance.

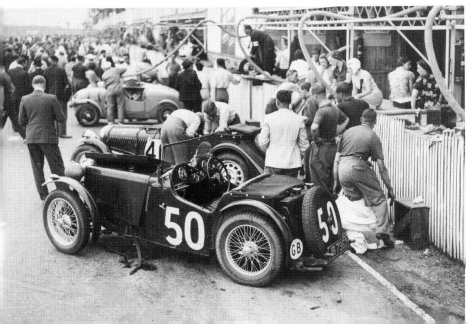

MG, No.50. Driven by Mrs Wisdom/Dobson. This car retired during the 48th lap with engine overheating after completing 402.41 miles in nine hours of racing.

1939

This was Bugatti's last victory, won in the face of stiff competition – Lagonda tried hard for a second victory. The two French drivers Wimille and Veyron completed 2084.55 miles. This race marked the end of an epoch at Le Mans as, two months later, the Second World War broke out.

Aston Martin, No.29. Driven by Hitchens/Morris-Goodall. This car was placed a very creditable twelfth on distance after completing 1670.34 miles in 24 hours at an average speed of 69.60mph. One of this Aston's fastest laps was timed at 6min 6.9sec – an average speed of 82.22mph.

Aston Martin, No.31. Driven by Polledry/Robert and retired during the 155th lap after completing 1299.45 miles in almost thirteen hours of racing. Before it retired this Aston had been timed at 6min 38.4sec – an average speed of 75.72mph.

MG, No.36. Driven by Collier/Welch. This car, the thirteenth retirement of the race, was timed at 6min 58.4sec; an average speed of 71.77mph before it too retired during the 63rd lap with a leaking fuel tank, having completed 528.16 miles.

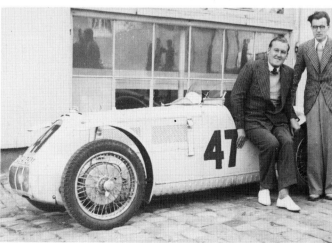

MG, No.47. Driven by Bonneau/Mathieu. This car retired during the 40th lap after completing only 335.34 miles. Prior to this, the Franco-Belgian team (Bonneau was Belgian, Mathieu, French) had been clocked at 63.44mph or a lap in 7min 55.9sec.

1949

As a sign of the times, a 2-litre Ferrari won the first Le Mans 24 Hour race to be held after the war. Chinetti and Selsdon, however, were not able to improve on the 1939 record set by Bugatti. They completed 1974.90 miles at an average speed of 82.28mph.

Aston Martin DB2, No.19. Entered by Aston Martin Lagonda and driven by Johnson/Brackenbury. This was the first British team to retire from the race (with cooling problems after only six laps and 50.301 miles). This 'Works' Aston, the only one to be entered by the factory, was alone in being fitted with a six-cylinder engine.

Aston Martin DB1, No.27. Entered by A.W. Jones and driven by Jones/Haines. This car was placed seventh on distance after completing 1740.56 miles in 24 hours at an average speed of 72.52mph. In addition it was placed eighth in the Index of Performance and third in the 1501 – 2000cc class.

Aston Martin DB1, No.28. Entered by Mrs R.P. Hitchens and driven by Maréchal/Mathieson. This Aston was involved in an accident on the 193rd lap which, sadly, was to prove fatal for Maréchal who died of his injuries in hospital.

Aston Martin DB1, No.29. Entered by R. Lawrie and driven by Lawrie/Parker. This Aston was placed eleventh on distance after completing 1625.95 miles in 24 hours at an average speed of 67.75mph. This car finished particularly well and was twelfth in the Index of Performance.

Bentley, No.6. Entered by H.S.F. Hay and driven by Hay/Wisdom. This car was placed sixth on distance after completing 1765.55 miles in 24 hours at an average speed of 73.56mph. Hay had been one of the first competitors to enter when the post-war revival of the Le Mans 24 Hours was announced and, good husband that he was, had chosen his wife as co-driver. In the event, however 'Tommy' Wisdom took her place. This was an excellent placing for this car which had been entered as a Rolls-Bentley.

Aston Martin DB1, No.31. Entered by Dudley Folland and driven by Heal/Folland. Like its team-mate, No.19, this Aston suffered from cooling problems which forced it to retired at 7.30pm after completing only 26 laps and 217.48 miles.

Aston Martin DB1, No.30. Entered by R.P. Monkhouse and driven by Monkhouse/Stapleton. La Sarthe obviously had the effect of making Aston Martins overheat! No.30 had completed 45 laps when cooling problems forced retirement at 10.21pm.

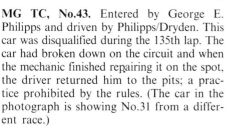

MG TC, No.43. Entered by George E. Philipps and driven by Philipps/Dryden. This car was disqualified during the 135th lap. The car had broken down on the circuit and when the mechanic finished repairing it on the spot, the driver returned him to the pits; a practice prohibited by the rules. (The car in the photograph is showing No.31 from a different race.)

Healey Saloon, No.20. Entered by Jack Bartlett and driven by Bartlett/Mann. This car was placed thirteenth on distance after completing 1515.63 miles in 24 hours at an average speed of 63.15mph.

1950

This year saw Talbot's only victory at Le Mans and the great Louis Rosier was well rewarded for having driven for the entire race, bar two laps. Louis and his co-driver, son Jean-Louis, completed 2153.13 miles in 24 hours at an average speed of 89.71mph. There were 60 cars at the start including three from Jaguar, making its début at Le Mans.

Aston Martin DB1, No.19. Entered by Aston Martin Lagonda and driven by Abecassis/Macklin. This car was placed fifth on distance after completing 2094.17 miles in 24 hours at an average speed of 87.26mph.

During the 23rd hour, this Aston was on a par with the Montrémy/Hémard Monopole-Panhard in the Index of Performance; the Aston only had to accelerate to win. Unfortunately for the British team, the Aston's engine started to misfire and the car ran out of fuel in the penultimate lap and was overtaken by the little Monopole. No.19 was, however, able to finish, was still equal first in the Index of Performance and won the 3-litre class. In the evening after the race, George Abecassis returned to his hotel to find a telegram announcing the birth of his fourth child.

Aston Martin DB2, No.20. Registration UMC 66. Entered by Aston Martin Lagonda and driven by Fairman/Thompson. This car retired after three hours.

In those far off and more relaxed days, cars travelled to Le Mans by road. During the journey, Jack Fairman had an accident at Brionne, in Normandy, and although his own injuries were slight, his wife Marion, who was driving with him, was taken to hospital.

As it was no longer possible to race the car (registration no VMF 65), it was replaced by a 'mule' (service car) to avoid the customary fine of 10000 francs levied for 'no-shows'.

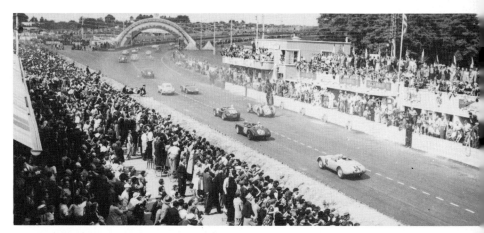

Aston Martin DB2, No.21. Chassis No. LML/50/7, registration VMF 63. Entered by Aston Martin Lagonda and driven by Brackenbury/Parnell. This car was placed sixth on distance after completing 2046.99 miles in 24 hours at average speed of 85.30mph.

John Wyer, the Aston team manager, had targeted a speed of 5min 45sec per lap. This DB2, a slower car than that driven by Abecassis and Macklin, was, nevertheless, very well placed; it was sixth overall, second in the 3-litre class and third in the Index of Performance.

Nash-Healey, No.14. Driven by Rolt/Hamilton. This car was placed fourth on distance after completing 2103.27 miles in 24 hours at an average speed of 87.64mph. It was also eighth in the Index of Performance and came third in the 5-litre class.

Healey Silverstone, No.23. Driven by Mann/Morris-Goodall. This car was placed nineteenth on distance after completing 1706.65 miles in 24 hours at an average speed of 71.11mph. It was also placed 28th (second to last) in the Index of Performance. The Healey shown in the photograph is not the one raced.

Bentley, No.11. Driven by Hall/Clarke. This Bentley was placed eighth on distance after completing 1990.83 miles in 24 hours at an average speed of 82.95mph.

Bentley, No.12. Driven by Hay/Hunter. This car was placed fourteenth on distance after completing 1886.55 miles in 24 hours at an average speed of 78.61mph. It is said that this 'old' Bentley already had some 125,000 miles on the clock before taking part in this race; nevertheless it acquitted itself very well.

MG, No.39. Driven by Philipps/Winterbottom. This MG was placed eighteenth on distance after completing 1747.66 miles in 24 hours at an average speed of 72.82mph and was thirteenth in the Index of Performance.

Jaguar XK120, No.15. Driven by Clark/Haines. This car was placed twelfth on distance after completing 1946.90 miles in 24 hours at an average speed of 81.12mph.

Jaguar XK120, No.16. Driven by Whitehead/Marshall. This car was placed fifteenth on distance after completing 1836.31 miles in 24 hours at an average speed of 78.60mph and was twentieth in the Index of Performance.

Jaguar XK120, No.17. Registration JWK 651. Driven by Johnson/Hadley. This car retired in the 23rd hour although it was in seventh place during the preceding hour. At the end of the night this very fast but unlucky Jaguar had been second on distance. Leslie Johnson, when asked why the car was painted white, joked that as he was a Scot he had economised on green paint.

1951

Jaguar celebrated its first victory in this Le Mans 24 Hour Race, the first page in a dramatic story that is not yet fully told. There were 60 cars at the start including a large number of British marques: Jaguar, of course; Aston Martin, Healey, Frazer Nash, Bentley (not present in 1950), Jowett, Allard and MG.

Aston Martin DB2, No.24. Registration XMC 76. Entered by Aston Martin Lagonda and driven by Parnell/Hampshire. This car was placed seventh on distance after completing 2113.65 miles in 24 hours at an average speed of 88.07mph.

Aston Martin DB2, No.25. Registration XMC 77. Entered by Aston Martin Lagonda and driven by Abecassis/Shawe-Taylor. This car was placed fifth on distance after completing 2143.29 miles in 24 hours at an average speed of 89.30mph and was second in the 3-litre class.

Aston Martin DB2, No.26. Registration VMF 64. Entered by Aston Martin Lagonda and driven by Macklin/Thompson. This Aston was placed third on distance after completing 2160.45 miles in 24 hours at an average speed of 90.02mph. This 'sports saloon' won the 3-litre class and was fourth in the Index of Performance. Although placed only third overall, this car broke the race record established the previous year by Rosier's victorious Talbot.

Aston Martin DB2, No.27. Entered by Aston Martin Lagonda and driven by Clark/Scott. This car was placed thirteenth on distance after completing 1958.58 miles in 24 hours at an average speed of 81.62mph.

Aston Martin DB2, No.28. Entered by Aston Martin Lagonda and driven by Mann/Morris-Goodall. This car was placed tenth on distance after completing 1956.11 miles in 24 hours at an average speed of 82.75mph.

Nash-Healey, No.19. Driven by Rolt/Hamilton. This Healey was placed sixth on distance after completing 2142.94 miles in 24 hours at an average speed of 89.29mph.

Jaguar XK120C, No.20. Entered by Jaguar Cars and driven by Walker/Whitehead. This car was placed first on distance after completing 2243.89 miles in 24 hours at an average speed of 93.50mph. The consistent driving by the two Peters was rewarded by their success in this race.

Jaguar XK120C, No.21. Registration AEN 546. Entered by Jaguar Cars and driven by Lawrie/Walker. This car was placed eleventh on distance after completing 1980.44 miles in 24 hours at an average speed of 82.51mph.

Jaguar C-type, No.22. Entered by Jaguar Cars and driven by Moss/Fairman. This C-type Jaguar had to retire although it had been in first place at one time. A new lap record of 4min 46.8sec or 105.23mph was set by the spirited Stirling Moss.

Jaguar XK120C, No.23. Driven by Johnson/Biondetti and retired after 50 laps.

1952

Bentley, No.14. Driven by Hay/Clark. This car was placed 22nd on distance after completing 1718.17 miles in 24 hours at an average speed of 71.60mph.

MG, No.43. Driven by Philipps/Rippon and retired with a damaged piston.

Aston Martin DB2, No.32. Entered by Peter Clark and driven by Clark/Keen. This Aston was placed seventh on distance after completing 2072.76 miles in 24 hours at an average speed of 86.36mph and was also placed third in the 3-litre class (behind two Mercedes) and tenth in the Index of Performance. This Aston was fitted with four SU carburettors.

After an abortive attempt at the beginning of the Thirties, Mercedes finally met with victory at Le Mans with the highly successful 300SL, which took first and second in 1952.

Mercedes broke the record by completing 2344.93 miles at an average speed of 96.67mph. There were another 55 cars at the start but none of them hindered the German duo.

Aston Martin DB3, No.25. Entered by Aston Martin Lagonda and driven by Macklin/Collins. This car retired in the 22nd hour although earlier in the race it had been placed fourth. Different authorities suggest different reasons for this car's retirement. Whatever the reason, this Works Aston, driven by two top-class drivers, ran a fine race.

Aston Martin DB3, No.27. Entered by Aston Martin Lagonda and driven by Parnell/Thompson. This Aston retired at 4.45pm with transmission problems.

Aston Martin DB3, No.26. Entered by Aston Martin Lagonda and driven by Poore/Griffith. This car retired during the third hour; it had been in 27th place during the preceding hour. Pat Griffith replaced George Abecassis in this race. The DB3 retired as a result of a damaged water pump at 6.59pm.

Aston Martin DB2, No.31. Entered by Nigel Mann and driven by Mann/Morris-Goodall. This car retired during the sixteenth hour after being placed twentieth during the preceding hour. A flat battery resulting from a broken dynamo mounting was responsible for this retirement at 7.05am.

Jaguar C-type, No.17. Entered by Peter Walker and driven by Moss/Walker. This car retired in the third hour and had been placed eighth during the preceding hour. Severe cooling problems, which were not alleviated by the mechanics fitting a bigger radiator, resulted in engine failure at 6.03pm from a run big end. No.18 was also refitted with a larger radiator with equally unsuccessful results.

Jaguar C-type, No.18. Entered by Jaguar Cars and driven by Rolt/Hamilton. This Jaguar retired after four hours and had been placed 36th an hour earlier. Like the two other Jaguars, No.18 suffered from cooling problems, culminating in this case with a blown cylinder head gasket at 7.00pm. The engines of these three Jaguars developed 200bhp.

Jaguar C-type, No.19. Entered by Jaguar Cars and driven by Whitehead/Stewart. Jaguar No.19 retired during the second hour at 5.55pm and had been placed eighth at the end of the first hour. This was the first of the Jaguars to retire and like the others suffered from overheating. This was the result of the new bodywork design which did not provide the airflow necessary at high speeds. As on No.18, the cylinder head gasket blew.

1953

Jaguar unexpectedly snatched victory from under the nose of favourites Ferrari and Alfa Romeo and in so doing broke the 170km/h average speed barrier. The best Ferrari could manage was fifth after three Jaguars and an American Cunningham. There were 60 entries in this race.

Aston Martin DB3S, No.25. Engine No. DP 101/20. Entered by Aston Martin Lagonda and driven by Parnell/Collins. This car was retired during the second hour when, with Reg Parnell (seen behind the car in overalls) driving, it left the road and was too badly damaged to continue.

Aston Martin DB3S, No.26. Engine No. DP 101/21. Entered by Aston Martin Lagonda and driven by Salvadori/Abecassis. This Aston retired during the tenth hour with clutch failure.

Aston Martin DB2, No.69. Chassis No. LML 50/57, engine No. LB 6V50 339. Peter Clark and Tom Meyer had to drive this virtually obsolete supercharged Aston which found itself first reserve behind the Fiat V8 which only completed a few laps.

Aston Martin DB3S, No.27. Engine No. DP 101/22. Entered by Aston Martin Lagonda and driven by Poore/Thompson. This car retired during the eighteenth hour with valve problems.

Austin-Healey 100, No.33. Chassis No. SPL/226/B, engine No.1B 136 903, registration NOJ 391. Driven by Becquart/Wilkins. This Healey was placed fourteenth on distance after completing 2101.26 miles in 24 hours at an average speed of 87.55mph, third in the 3-litre class and 24th in the Index of Performance.

Austin-Healey 100, No.34. Chassis No. X15, engine No. 1B 136 876. Driven by Gatsonides/Lockett. This car was placed twelfth on distance after completing 2151.60 miles in 24 hours at an average speed of 89.65mph. A contemporary source remarked on a brilliant race run by the two Healeys, commenting on the fact that they were without doubt the least expensive cars at Le Mans and essentially standard.
No.34 finished second in the 3-litre class and 22nd in the Index of Performance.

Jaguar C-type, No.20. Engine No. E 1047. Entered by Jacques Swaters/Écurie Francorchamps and driven by Laurent/de Tornaco. This car was placed ninth on distance after completing 2300.82 miles in 24 hours at an average speed of 95.87mph.

Jaguar C-type, No.19. Engine No. E 1054, registration 194 WK. Entered by Jaguar Cars and driven by Whitehead/Stewart. This car was placed fourth on distance after completing 2485.90 miles at an average speed of 103.58mph and was also seventh in the Index of Performance and third in its class. At the time, *Autosport* published a list of honour of the Jaguar mechanics who contributed so much to the Jaguar victory.

Jaguar C-type, No.18. Engine No. E 1053, registration 774 RW. Entered by Jaguar Cars and driven by Rolt/Hamilton. This car was placed first on distance after completing 2540.58 miles in 24 hours at an average speed of 105.84mph. This was the superb victory England had been waiting for since 1951 and at Le Mans, one victory is usually followed by another. The driving throughout the race was of exceptionally high standard and breaking the 4,000km (2485 miles) distance barrier put the icing on the cake for Rolt and Hamilton who also won third place in the Index of Performance.

Jaguar C-type, No.17. Engine No. E 1055, registration 164 WK. Entered by Jaguar Cars and driven by Moss/Walker. This Jaguar was placed second on distance after completing 2511.08 miles in 24 hours at an average speed of 104.63mph. Jaguar No.17 was in first place at the end of the first hour but had to stop in the 19th and 22nd laps. It took all of the drivers' talent to claw their way back into the race and to achieve this very creditable second place. All competitors were given the option of using straight pump petrol at 90 octane or petrol-benzole-alcohol blend. Of the 26 starters, seventeen ran on standard fuel including the Jaguars.

The 24 Hours of 1954 was a particularly exciting, closely run race which put Ferrari into the annals of motoring history along with two very different drivers: Gonzalez and Trintignant. The winning distance and average speed, 2523.48 miles and 105.145mph, respectively, had dropped slightly but this did nothing to diminish Ferrari's victory. Jaguar, however disappointed, were undeterred in the sure knowledge that one Le Mans victory is generally followed by another.

Aston Martin DB3S, No.8. Chassis No. DB 3S 1, engine No. DP 101/17, registration YMF 307. Entered by David Brown and driven by Parnell/Salvadori. This car retired during the 21st hour. This Aston, driven by the unlucky Reg Parnell, stopped after only 5 miles before leaving again to return to the pits at 4.15am. It was officially retired at 11.50am with supercharger problems as the probable cause.

Aston Martin DB3S, No.20. Chassis No. DB 3S 6, engine No. DP 101/36. Entered by David Brown and driven by Collins/Bira. This Aston retired at 4.15am after an accident.

Aston Martin DB3S, No.21. Chassis No. DB 3S 7, engine No. DP 101/37. Entered by David Brown and driven by (G) Whitehead/Stewart. This car retired at 10.15pm after an accident involving car No.19, a Gordini.

Aston Martin DB3S, No.22. Chassis No. DB 3S 3, engine No. DP 101/18. Entered by David Brown and driven by Shelby/Frère. This Aston retired 26 minutes after midnight with damage to the front off-side stub axle and wheel bearing.

Aston Martin DB2/4, No.27. Chassis No. LML 693, engine No. VB 69 132, registration 1853 TT 75. Entered by J.P. Colas and driven by Colas/Da Silva Ramos. This car retired during the fourteenth hour with transmission problems.

Triumph TR2, No.62. Chassis No. TS 1730.0, engine No. TS 1364 E, registration OKV 777. Entered by E.B. Wadsworth and driven by Wadsworth/Brown. This car was placed fifteenth on distance after completing 1793.21 miles in 24 hours at an average speed of 74.72mph.

Jaguar D-type, No.15. Chassis No. XKC 404, engine No. E 2005/9, registration OKV 3. Entered by Jaguar Cars and driven by (P) Whitehead/Wharton. This Jaguar retired with gearbox problems at 3.24am. Like Jaguar No.14, this car also had trouble with spark plugs.

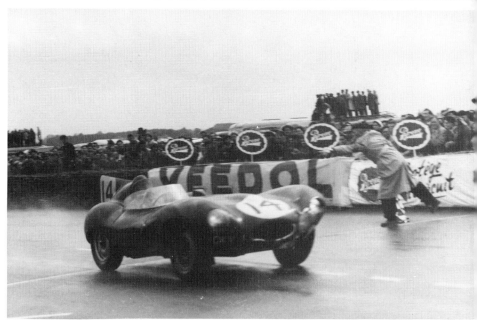

Jaguar D-type, No.14. Chassis No. XKC 402, engine No. E 2004/9, registration OKV 1. Entered by Jaguar Cars and driven by Rolt/Hamilton. This Jaguar was placed second on distance after completing 2520.94 miles at an average speed of 105.04mph and finished third in the Index of Performance. Early in the race minor problems – rectified by a change of spark plugs and petrol filter – slowed down this car. Nevertheless, Jaguar No.14 put up an impressive fight against Ferrari, the winners, and British honour.

Jaguar D-type, No.12. Chassis No. XKC 403, engine No. E 2003/9, registration OKV 2. Entered by Jaguar Cars and driven by Moss/Walker. Jaguar No.12 retired during the twelfth hour with a damaged brake circuit. This brilliant duo had already been held up with clutch problems for an hour and a half and with lighting problems for twenty minutes. In addition, they left the road at Mulsanne at 11.57pm.

Jaguar C-type, No.16. Engine No. E 1047/9, registration 40 431. Entered by Écurie Francorchamps and driven by Laurent/Swaters. This Jaguar was placed fourth on distance after completing 2314.68 miles in 24 hours at an average speed of 96.44mph. This car also took sixth place in the Index of Performance and third place in the 5-litre class.

1955

Nineteen fifty-five was a black year at Le Mans. Eighty-one people were the victims of a terrible accident involving Levegh in a Mercedes, Hawthorn in a Jaguar and Macklin in an Austin-Healey. As a result, the expected confrontation between Mercedes, Ferrari and Jaguar did not take place: Mercedes withdrew; Ferrari had lost form and Jaguar achieved a tragic victory.

Aston Martin DB3S, No.25. Chassis No. DB 3S 8, engine No. DP 101/11. Entered by Aston Martin Lagonda/M. Gatsonides and driven by Brooks/Riseley Pritchard. This car retired with a cracked battery during the ninth hour.

Aston Martin DB3S, No.24. Chassis No. DB 3S 7, engine No. DP 101/41, registration 63 EMU. Entered by Aston Martin Lagonda and driven by Salvadori/Walker. This car retired during the tenth hour with engine failure.

Aston Martin DB3S, No.23. Chassis No. DB 3S 6, engine No. DP 101/9, registration 62 EMU. Entered by Aston Martin Lagonda and driven by Collins/Frère. This car was placed second on distance after completing 2530.86 miles in 24 hours at an average speed of 105.45mph and won the 3-litre class.

Austin-Healey 100S, No.26. Chassis No. SPL 226 B, engine No. 261 BN, registration NOJ 393. Entered by Lance Macklin and driven by Macklin/Leston. This car, which had been placed 50th an hour earlier, retired as a result of the accident.

Jaguar D-type, No.6. Registration 774 RW. Entered by Jaguar Cars and driven by Hawthorn/Bueb. This Jaguar was placed first on distance after completing 2569.61 miles at an average speed of 107.08mph. Despite the tragedy, this was a victory nonetheless for Jaguar No.6 which, with Hawthorn at the wheel, broke the lap record and was second in the Index of Performance.

Jaguar D-type, No.7. Entered by Jaguar Cars and driven by Rolt/Hamilton. This Jaguar retired after sixteen hours and had been placed fifth an hour earlier. Retirement has been put down to two causes, a leaking fuel tank and gearbox failure.

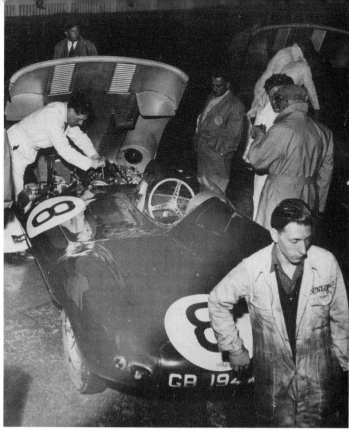

Jaguar D-type, No.8. Chassis No. XKD 508, engine No. E 3005, registration 194 WK. Entered by Jaguar Cars and driven by Beauman/Dewis. This car retired during the eleventh hour and had gone well until it got bogged down in the off-field sand. Its position each hour was as follows: 8, 8, 6, 5, 5, 4, 4, 4, 13, 15.

Jaguar D-type, No.9. Chassis No. XKD 507, engine No. E 3004/9. Entered by Briggs Cunningham and driven by Walters/Spear. This car retired after seven hours after being placed 48th an hour earlier. Ignition problems were responsible for the retirement of this American team.

Jaguar D-type, No.10. Chassis No. XKD 503, engine No. E 2011/9. Entered by Écurie Francorchamps and driven by Swaters/Claes. This car was placed third on distance after completing 2477.36 miles in 24 hours at an average speed of 103.16mph. It was also second in the 5-litre class and sixth in the Index of Performance.

MG EX182, No.41. Entered by MG and driven by Miles/Lockett. This MG was placed twelfth on distance after completing 2084.02 miles in 24 hours at an average speed of 86.83mph and was fifth in the 1500cc class. **MG EX182, No.42.** Entered by MG and driven by Jacobs/Flynn. This car had to retire after leaving the track during the sixth hour. **MG EX182, No.64.** Entered by MG and driven by Lund/Waeffler. This car was placed seventeenth on distance after completing 1961.20 miles at an average speed of 81.72mph.

Lotus IX, No.48. Chassis No. MK9/87, engine No. FWA 6300, registration XPE 6. Entered by Lotus Cars and driven by Chapman/Flockhart. This car was disqualified during the twelfth hour after being in 27th place an hour earlier.

Triumph TR2, No.28. Chassis No. TS 5534/0, engine No. TS 6062 E, registration PKV 376. Entered by Triumph and driven by Dickson/Sanderson. This car was placed fourteenth on distance after completing 2027.73 miles in 24 hours at an average speed of 84.49mph.

Triumph TR2, No.29. Chassis No. C 55 82, engine No. TS 5664 E, registration PKV 375. Entered by Triumph and driven by Hadley/Richardson. This car was placed fifteenth on distance after completing 2027.63 miles in 24 hours at an average speed of 84.48mph. The two Triumphs, Nos. 28 and 29, finished the race with only 175 yards between them.

Triumph TR2, No.68. Chassis No. TS 5691, engine No. TS 5749 E, registration PKV 374. Entered by Triumph and driven by Brooke/Morris-Goodall. This car was placed nineteenth on distance after completing 1793.05 miles at an average speed of 74.71mph.

1956

This was Jaguar's fourth Le Mans victory and it was a very open race. Of the fourteen cars placed, there were eleven different marques representing four different countries: Britain, Italy, Germany and France. After the previous year's catastrophe, the track had been modified, with particular attention given to the pit straight.

Aston Martin DB3S, No.8. Chassis No. DB3S 9, engine No. DP/101/H45. Entered by David Brown and driven by Moss/Collins. This car was placed second on distance after completing 2497.06 miles in 24 hours at an average speed of 104.04mph.
This particularly brilliant partnership battled against the winning Jaguar for first place for the whole 24 hours and finished only 10 miles behind its more powerful rival. At the beginning of the race, Moss was the fastest starter and he and Collins continued the struggle against the Écurie Écosse for the entire race. The car was timed at 146.07mph.

Aston Martin DBR1/250, No.14. Chassis No. MP 4013/1, engine No. RP 5053/L. Entered by David Brown and driven by Brooks/Parnell. This car had to retire during the 24th hour and had been in seventh place an hour earlier.
A damaged back axle brought the car to a halt near to Mulsanne and not far from the finishing line. The car had achieved fourth place during the night. This Aston achieved a speed of 131.05mph on the Mulsanne Straight.

Aston Martin DB3S, No.9. Engine No. DP 101/H41. Entered by David Brown and driven by Walker/Salvadori. This Aston retired in the sixteenth hour and had been in eighth position an hour earlier. Walker had just passed the grandstands and reached the Dunlop bridge in the pouring rain. He crashed into the right-hand barrier, careered across the track, to hit the left-hand barrier before finally ending up upside down in the middle of the track. Walker was taken to the Delagénière clinic with bruising and cuts on his face.

Jaguar D-type, No.1. Chassis No. XKD 605, engine No. E 4007, registration 393 RW. Entered by Jaguar Cars and driven by Hawthorn/Bueb. This Jaguar was placed sixth on distance after completing 2336.28 miles in 24 hours at an average speed of 97.35mph. Mike Hawthorn had to stop after only three laps with fuel injection problems; after several more stops, sand was detected in the filters and the problem rectified.

Hawthorn gave the Le Mans spectators a superb run for their money as he repeatedly attempted to break the lap record. He finally achieved this and established a new record of 4min 20sec and an average speed of 115.81mph; this was on the newly revised circuit.

Jaguar D-type, No.2. Chassis No. XKD 606, engine No. E 4006, registration 774 RW. Entered by Jaguar Cars and driven by Frère/Titterington. This car had to retire after an accident in the first lap which put two of the three Works Jaguars out of the race. It seems that this car had been entered at Le Mans with the registration 032 RW.

Jaguar D-type, No.3. Chassis No. XKD 602, engine No. E 404, registration 351 RW. Entered by Jaguar Cars and driven by Fairman/Wharton. During the first lap, Jack Fairman collided with Paul Frère in the Esses at Tertre Rouge. He crashed into the barriers but managed to get off again before he, in turn, was hit by De Portago in a Ferrari. Fairman returned the D-type to the pits but it was too badly damaged to be repaired. This Jaguar was fitted with Lucas fuel injection.

Jaguar D-type, No.5. Chassis No. XKD 573, engine No. E 2079/9, registration 164 WK. Entered by L'Équipe Nationale Belge and driven by Swaters/Rousselle. This Jaguar was placed fourth on distance after completing 2371.57 miles at an average speed of 98.82mph.
  Consistent driving brought success for this yellow Jaguar which was tenth in the Index of Performance, and was the second Jaguar to finish, taking second place in the 5-litre class.

Jaguar XK140, No.6. Chassis No. S 804 231, engine No. G 4060/9S, registration PWT 846. Entered by Robert Walshaw and driven by Walshaw/Bolton. This Jaguar which had been in eleventh place an hour earlier, was disqualified at 12 noon for refuelling in the 203rd lap instead of the 204th. In spite of injunctions to stop, the Jaguar continued nonetheless for another hour and a quarter.

Lotus Eleven, No.35. Chassis No. MK11/211, engine No. FWA/400/7/6804, registration DEC 494. Entered by Lotus Engineering and driven by Allison/Hall. This car was retired during the tenth hour and had been in seventeenth place an hour earlier.
Cliff Allison ran into a large dog which damaged the Lotus so badly that the car was forced to retire.

Jaguar D-type, No.4. Engine No. E 2036/9, registration MWS 301. Entered by Écurie Écosse and driven by Sanderson/Flockhart. This Jaguar D-type was placed first on distance after completing 2507.19 miles in 24 hours at an average speed of 104.47mph. Driving an unmodified D-type, identical to that in the D-type sales catalogue, Sanderson and Flockhart, who were managed brilliantly by David Murray, won a particularly gruelling Le Mans. Consistent driving in both wet and dry conditions as well as sheer speed contributed to this splendid victory.

The Jaguar reached a maximum speed of 156.868mph on the Mulsanne Straight, was placed ninth in the Index of Performance and won the 5-litre class.

Lotus Eleven, No.32. Chassis No. MK11/212, engine No. FWB400/7/8/6631, registration 9 EXH. Entered by Lotus Engineering and driven by Chapman/Frazer. The car retired in the 21st hour, though only an hour earlier it was in eighteenth place.

The retirement occurred after 179 laps, the 83bhp Climax engine giving up the ghost 1200 metres from the grandstands. It was the 32nd retirement in this particularly ferocious race.

Lotus Eleven, No.36. Chassis No. MK11/210, engine No. FWA400/7/6793, registration XJ 1802. Entered by Lotus Engineering and driven by Bicknell/Jopp. The car completed 2111.21 miles in 24 hours at an average speed of 87.97mph and was placed seventh on distance.

Fourth in the Index of Performance and winner of the 1100cc category, this was a splendid victory for the last surviving Lotus after a long battle against the Cooper.

This driver had to stop to remove a newspaper, which had blown over the car's radiator. The Bicknell/Jopp car reached a maximum speed of 128.19mph.

1957

This supreme victory was Jaguar's last for many years and the pinnacle of the marque's success at Le Mans. Of the 54 starters, Ferrari and, indeed, Maserati, had been widely tipped to win. Like Bentley, Jaguar now had five Le Mans victories to its name.

AC Ace Bristol, No.31. Chassis No. BE205, engine No. 768, registration 170 DPC. Entered by Peter Bolton and driven by Rudd/Bolton. This car was placed tenth on distance after completing 2349.08 miles in 24 hours at an average speed of 97.88mph and finished second in the 5-litre class.

Aston Martin DBR2, No.5. Chassis No. DBR 2/1, engine No. RDP 5057/2. Entered by David Brown and driven by P. Whitehead/G. Whitehead. This car, which had been in nineteenth position an hour earlier, retired during the eighth hour. Gearbox problems forced the retirement of the Works Aston.

Aston Martin DBR1, No.20. Chassis No. DBR 1/2, engine No. RB6/300/2. Entered by David Brown and driven by Brooks/Cunningham-Reid. This car, which had been in sixth position an hour earlier, retired during the twelfth hour.
Shortly after refuelling at 2am, Tony Brooks, who had just taken the wheel, skidded on a bend at Tertre Rouge and Maglioli, driving a Porsche, cannoned into him from behind. The two drivers were taken to the Delagénière hospital but escaped with only minor injuries. This was the only Aston Martin to be involved in the fight for first place, and the accident left the field open for the Jaguars to take the first four places.

Aston Martin DBR1, No.19. Chassis No. DBR 1/1, engine No. RB6/300/1. Entered by David Brown and driven by Salvadori/Leston. This car retired during the tenth hour and had been in ninth place during the preceding hour. Clutch and gearbox problems were responsible for this retirement.

Aston Martin DB3S, No.21. Chassis No. DB 3S/117, engine No. VB 65 117, registration 2570 34. Entered by J.P. Colas and driven by Colas/Kerguen. This Aston was placed eleventh on distance after completing 2273.59 miles in 24 hours at an average speed of 94.73mph. This was the most successful Aston Martin in the race, winning the 3-litre class.

Jaguar D-type, No.3. Chassis No. XKD 606, engine No. E5005/9. Entered by Écurie Écosse and driven by Flockhart/Bueb. This Jaguar was placed first on distance after completing 2732.24 miles in 24 hours at an average speed of 113.85mph.
Bueb took the wheel at the beginning of the race, which was started by M. Chapalain, the Mayor of Le Mans. After two and a half hours of racing André Simon, who had taken over from Jean Behra in the leading Maserati, broke down with transmission problems and left the field open to Jaguar No.3 which took the lead and won fifth place in the Index of Performance.

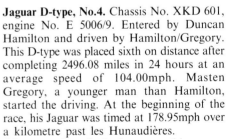

Jaguar D-type, No.4. Chassis No. XKD 601, engine No. E 5006/9. Entered by Duncan Hamilton and driven by Hamilton/Gregory. This D-type was placed sixth on distance after completing 2496.08 miles in 24 hours at an average speed of 104.00mph. Masten Gregory, a younger man than Hamilton, started the driving. At the beginning of the race, his Jaguar was timed at 178.95mph over a kilometre past les Hunaudières.
After a number of misadventures, this car ran off the track and got stuck in the sand at Arnage during the eighteenth hour which slowed it still further.

Jaguar D-type, No.15. Chassis No. XKD 60[?] engine No. E 4007. Entered by Écurie Écos[se] and driven by Sanderson/Lawrence. Th[e] Jaguar was placed second on distance afte[r] completing 2665.39 miles in 24 hours at a[n] average speed of 111.06mph and was eight[h] in the Index of Performance.

Jaguar D-type, No.16. Chassis No. XKD 57[?] engine No. E 2079/9, registration NKV 479[?] Entered by the Équipe Nationale Belge an[d] driven by Frère/Rousselle. This Jaguar wa[s] placed fourth on distance after completin[g] 2590.64 miles in 24 hours at an average spee[d] of 107.94mph.
Lucien Bianchi had originally been expecte[d] to drive this Belgian Jaguar, which was place[d] eleventh in the Index of Performance and wa[s] clocked at 160.82mph on the Mulsann[e] Straight.

Lotus Eleven, No.55. Chassis No. MK11/323[?] engine No. FWA 7134, registration XAR 11[?] Entered by Lotus Engineering and driven b[y] Allison/Hall. This Lotus was placed four[-] teenth on distance after completing 2160.6[?] miles in 24 hours at an average speed o[f] 90.03mph. This 745cc car won the Index o[f] Performance and the 750cc class.
From the first hours of the race, this Lotu[s] was engaged in a battle for the Index with[?] the DB No.50 and the Osca No.46. With [a] top speed of 114.31mph, recorded on th[e] Mulsanne Straight, the Lotus responded with[?] spirit to the challenge of France and Italy[.]

Jaguar D-type, No.17. Chassis No. XKD 513[?] engine No. E2022/9. Entered by H. Peignau[x] and driven by Lucas/'Mary' (Pierre Brousse[l]let). This Jaguar was placed third on distanc[e] after completing 2644.03 miles in 24 hours a[t] an average speed of 110.17mph. This blu[e] Jaguar, which was not fitted with a tail-fin[,] was placed ninth in the Index of Performance[.]

Lotus Eleven, No.41. Chassis No. MK11/320[?] engine No. FWA 7125, registration YAR 527[?] Entered by A. Héchard and driven b[y] Héchard/Masson. This car was placed six[-] teenth on distance after completing 2110.1[?] miles in 24 hours at an average speed o[f] 87.92mph.
This car came close to retiring when it ra[n] out of fuel at 6.45pm at Mulsanne. Roge[r] Masson, who was driving, pushed the Lotu[s] to the pits where he had to treat the soles o[f] his feet which had been burnt by the ho[t] tarmac.

Lotus Eleven, No.42. Chassis No. MK11/321, engine No. FWA 7128, registration UDV 609. Entered by P. Walshaw and driven by Walshaw/Dalton. This car was placed thirteenth on distance after completing 2161.02 miles in 24 hours at an average speed of 90.04mph. A diversion into the barrier just before the S-bends at Tertre Rouge did not manage to stop this little Lotus which was tenth in the Index of Performance.

Lotus Eleven, No.62. Chassis No. MK11/324, engine No. FWA 7.7126, registration DEC 494. Entered by Lotus Engineering and driven by Frazer/Chamberlain. This Lotus was placed ninth on distance after completing 2377.99 miles in 24 hours at an average speed of 99.09mph.

No.62 was second in the Index of Performance, first in the 1100cc class and was timed at 133.95mph.

1958

There were fifty starters at this, the 26th Le Mans 24 Hour Race which was won for the third time by Ferrari. Porsche put up a serious challenge, three of their RS coming in the first five. The winning drivers were Olivier Gendebien and Phil Hill who completed 2548.82 miles at an average speed of 106.20mph. The race record, however, still unbroken, remained with Jaguar.

AC Ace Bristol, No.27. Chassis No. BEX 399, engine No. 100 D2/S870, registration NE 17376. Entered by Écurie Trois Chevrons/Neuchâtel and driven by Patthey/Berger. This car was placed ninth on distance after completing 2129.20 miles in 24 hours at an average speed of 88.72mph. There were two Aces in the race, and they finished one behind the other with the English-owned car ahead of the Swiss.

AC Ace Bristol, No.28. Chassis No. LM 5000, engine No. 100/D2 S 860, registration 8 FPK. Entered by William Hurlock and driven by Bolton/Stoop. This Ace was placed eighth on distance after completing 2143.65 miles in 24 hours at an average speed of 89.32mph. This AC had special bodywork.

Aston Martin DBR1, No.3. Chassis No. DBR 1/2, engine No. RB6/300/1. Entered by David Brown and driven by Brooks/Trintignant. This Aston, which had been in third place an hour earlier, retired during the fifteenth hour. At 5.50am, Maurice Trintignant was forced to retire at Mulsanne with failed transmission. This was particularly unfortunate as the Anglo-French team had been holding third and fourth place in the race and were definitely in the running.

Aston Martin DBR1, No.2. Chassis No. DBR 1/3, engine No. RB6/300/3. Entered by David Brown and driven by Moss/Brabham. This Aston, which had been leading the field for the first two hours, retired at Mulsanne with engine failure in the third hour at 5.12pm. Stirling Moss started the 1958 Le Mans in great style, leading the race with Gendebien and Hawthorn in hot pursuit in their Ferraris. Moss' fastest lap took 4min 9.4sec, an average speed of 120.74mph.

Aston Martin DBR1, No.4. Chassis No. DBR 1/1, engine No. RB6/300/2. Entered by David Brown and driven by Salvadori/Lewis-Evans. This car, which had been in eighth place an hour earlier, was retired during the fourth hour. The Aston skidded in the unusually heavy rain and crashed into the barrier on the bend following the grandstands. This was the thirteenth retirement of the race.

Aston Martin DB3S, No.5. Chassis No. DB 3S/6, engine No. DP 101/36, registration 62 EMU. Entered by G. Whitehead and driven by P. Whitehead/G. Whitehead. This Aston was placed second on distance after completing 2448.75 miles in 24 hours at an average speed of 102.03mph.
Despite their speed, the Whitehead cousins had, in fact, been playing a waiting game and when Jaguar No.8 retired, seized their chance to snatch second place. They were also tenth in the Index of Performance.

Jaguar D-type, No.8. Chassis No. XKD 601, engine No. EE 1201/10, registration 2 CPG. Entered by Duncan Hamilton and driven by Hamilton/Bueb. This Jaguar retired in the twentieth hour after holding second place an hour earlier.
Hamilton drove a marvellous race, starting in sixth place in the first hour and gradually creeping up into first place during the eighth. From then on until his accident at 11.50am, he maintained a steady second place before leaving the track at Arnage in the pouring rain and coming to a halt after driving through a hedge.

Jaguar D-type, No.6. Chassis No. XKD 603, engine No. EE 1207/10, registration RSF 303. Entered by Écurie Écosse and driven by Fairman/Gregory. This Jaguar retired during the second hour with a broken piston. The car had been in 51st position during the first hour of the race.

Jaguar D-type, No.7. Chassis No. XKD 504, engine No. E 4007/10, registration RSF 302. Entered by Écurie Écosse and driven by Sanderson/Lawrence. This Jaguar was involved with Aston and Ferrari in the early skirmish for the lead, but broke a piston after only fifteen minutes and had to retire.

Lister, No.9. Chassis No. BHL 105. Engine No. EE 1204/10. Entered by the Équipe Nationale Belge and driven by Rousselle/Dubois. This car retired after oil pressure failure during the fourth hour after holding fifteenth place an hour earlier. Mauro Bianchi, then a race mechanic, is shown here at the wheel.

Lister, No.10. Chassis No. BHL 5, engine No. EE 1205/10, registration HCH 736. Entered by Bruce Halford and driven by Halford/Naylor. This Lister was placed fifteenth on distance after completing 2009.99 miles in 24 hours at an average speed of 83.74mph. The car came close to retirement when, at noon, the driver had to stop at Mulsanne to sort out a malfunctioning gearbox.

Jaguar D-type, No.11. Chassis No. XKD 513, engine No. EE 1208/10, registration 6478 AT 69. Entered by Henri Peignaux and driven by 'Mary'/Guelfi. Jaguar No.11, in 37th place during the preceding hour, retired during the seventh hour. The rain was responsible for this car skidding off the track; the driver, 'Mary', (*nom de course* of Pierre Brousselet) was severely injured and later died in the Delagénière clinic.

Jaguar D-type, No.57. Chassis No. XKD 502, engine No. 9200 E 2010/9, registration MWS 302. Entered by Maurice Charles and driven by Charles/Young. This Jaguar was retired in the third hour and had been in seventeenth place during the preceding hour.
A violent storm at the end of the second hour was responsible for the concertina-ing of this Jaguar driven by Maurice Charles, Lotus No.56 and the Panhard No.51. Charles was slightly injured and was taken off the course in an ambulance.

Lotus Fifteen, No.26. Chassis No. 608, engine No. 8/1067. Entered by Lotus Engineering and driven by Allison/G. Hill. This Works Lotus was retired during the second hour with engine failure caused by a faulty cooling system. The car had been in 53rd place during the first hour.

Lotus Eleven, No.55. Chassis No. MKXI 514, engine No. 726/1. Entered by Lotus Engineering and driven by Stacey/Dickson. This car was placed twentieth on distance after completing 1688.46 miles at an average speed of 70.35mph.

Dickson got stuck in the sand on the Mulsanne Curve and worked for two hours to extricate the little Lotus which finished last.

Lotus Eleven, No.38. Chassis No. MKXI 513, engine No. 400/7. Entered by Lotus Engineering and driven by Ireland/H. Taylor. This car, which had been in 21st place during the preceding hour, retired during the twentieth hour.

A head-to-tail collision in the pouring rain at the beginning of the race did not stop this 1100cc Lotus which finally retired at 7.20am on Sunday morning when the ignition failed.

Lotus Eleven, No.39. Chassis No. MKXI 519, registration POY 780. Entered by Car Exchange and driven by Frost/Hicks. This car retired in the third hour after an accident. It had been in 25th place during the preceding hour.

Lotus Fifteen, No.35. Chassis 607, engine No. 8/1054. Entered by Lotus Engineering and driven by Chamberlain/Lovely. The Lotus retired during the eighth hour and had been in 37th place during the preceding hour. This American team had to retire as a result of an accident; Chamberlain was slightly concussed.

Lotus Eleven, No.56. Chassis No. MKXI 9, engine No. 7/726/3. Entered by G. Crombac and driven by Masson/Héchard. The car retired during the fourth hour and had been in 45th place during the preceding hour. Héchard was driving through a storm when he was involved in a bumper-to-bumper shunt with Charles's Jaguar and Poch's Panhard. Crombac, who entered the Lotus and was himself a well-known competitor, went on to found *Sport Auto*.

1959

Aston Martin took first and second place at Le Mans in 1959; their only victory in the 24 hour race. Ferrari made a great showing and dominated the GT class with their superb 250 Testa Rossa. They took third, fourth, fifth and sixth places overall. The British entry was particularly strong with nineteen cars representing seven marques.

AC Ace Bristol, No.29. GT category. Chassis No. BE 214, engine No. 100 D 764, registration 650 BPK. Entered by Rudd Racing and driven by Whiteaway/Turner. This Ace was placed seventh on distance, after completing 2289.65 miles in 24 hours at an average speed of 95.38mph, and second in the 2-litre class.

Aston Martin DBR1, No.4. Sports. Chassis No. DBR 1/3, engine No. RB6/300/1. Entered by David Brown and driven by Moss/Fairman. This Aston retired during the sixth hour and had been in third place during the preceding hour. Stirling Moss led the first lap of the race with the Ferraris in his wake. Moss drove so fast and so well that he wore out Aston's potential adversaries before retiring with engine failure and leaving the field open to his team mates, Shelby and Salvadori.

Aston Martin DBR1, No.5. Sports category. Chassis No. DBR 1/2, engine No. RB6/300/6. Entered by David Brown and driven by Salvadori/Shelby. This Aston was placed first on distance after completing 2701.66 miles in 24 hours at an average speed of 112.57mph. During the night, the Aston, then following the Gendebien/P. Hill Ferrari, had to stop in the pits to attend to vibration. However, this fine car driven by the then little-known Texan from Dallas won the day. A truly exceptional team of mechanics was behind this victory. They were Hind and Smith, Creswick (fuel specialist) with Reg Parnell as Team Manager. Henry Taylor was reserve driver.

Aston Martin DBR1, No.6. Sports category. Chassis No. DBR 1/4, engine No. RB6/300/4. Entered by David Brown and driven by Trintignant/Frère. This Aston was placed second on distance after completing 2695.23 miles in 24 hours at an average speed of 112.31mph. This reserve car came close to winning the Le Mans 24 Hours.

All the works Aston Martin DBR1s were fitted with Plexiglas windscreens and during the race carried 180 litres of BP fuel and 22 litres of oil. Their six cylinders had dual ignition (twelve KLG 10 spark plugs). Two Lucas headlamps and two foglamps adorned each bonnet.

Aston Martin DBR1, No.7. Sports category. Chassis No. DBR 1/5, engine No. RB6/300/5, registration 900 BH. Entered by A.G. Whitehead and driven by G. Whitehead/Naylor. This Aston retired during the fifth hour and had been in thirteenth place during the preceding hour. The first mishap to this team occurred when the car left the track and Brian Naylor damaged his arm. The *coup de grâce* quickly followed when the Aston was involved in an accident with a Stanguellini and a Cooper, and after being wrecked caught fire.

Aston Martin DB4, No.21. GT category. Chassis No. DP 199/1, engine No. RDP/5061.2. Entered by Écurie des Trois Chevrons and driven by Patthey/Calderari. This Aston retired in the third hour and had been in fourth position the hour before. Engine failure quashed the hopes of the two drivers who had come from Neuchâtel to take part in the race.

Lister-Jaguar LM, No.2. Sports category. Chassis No. BHL 3, engine No. EE 1302/9. Entered by Brian Lister and driven by Hansen/Blond. This car retired with a damaged piston during the fifth hour and had been placed fourteenth the hour before.

Jaguar D-type, No.3. Sports category. Chassis No. XKD 603, engine No. EE 1303/9. Entered by Écurie Écosse and driven by Ireland/Gregory. The car retired during the eventh hour and had been in second place an hour before.
This car had been the best Jaguar in the race for some time and was involved in the contest for first place with Ferrari and Aston. Sadly, like the other Jaguars and the Lister, this, too, had to drop out with engine failure (piston).

Lotus Fifteen, No.30. Sports category. Chassis No. 3/626, engine No. 25/1160. Entered by Team Lotus and driven by G. Hill/Jolly. This car retired in the tenth hour and had been in twelfth place an hour earlier.
A little after 5.30am, this Lotus stopped in the pits allowing Ireland's Jaguar, with which it had fought a duel, to fly past. Seventeen minutes later, Hill set off again but soon after was forced to retired with engine failure.

Lister-Jaguar LM, No.1. Sports category. Chassis No. BHL 2, engine No. EE 1305/9. Entered by Brian Lister and driven by Bueb/Halford. This car retired with engine failure during the ninth hour, having been in fourth place the hour before.

Lotus Elite, No.38. GT category. Chassis No. 1007, engine No. FWE 7540, registration 6 SME. Entered by Los Amigos and driven by Vidilles/Malle. This car retired during the tenth hour and had been in 21st place the hour before. This 'French' Lotus was completely destroyed by fire.

Lotus Elite, No.42. GT category. Chassis No. 1038, engine No. 15/7550. Entered by Border Reivers and driven by Clark/Whitmore. This car was placed tenth on distance after completing 2150.62 miles in 24 hours at an average speed of 89.61mph.

A pit stop early in the race followed by consistent driving resulted in tenth place for Jim Clark, future world champion, in his first (of three) Le Mans 24 hours races.

Lotus Fifteen, No.53. Sports category. Chassis No. 663, engine No. 441/2/3. Entered by Team Lotus and driven by Stacey/Green. This car retired during the fourteenth hour and had been in fourteenth place an hour earlier. Lotus No.53 was leading in the Index of Performance, ahead of Porsche, when a cylinder head gasket blew.

Triumph TR3, No.26. GT category. Chassis No. X 629, engine No. 737 E, registration XHP 940. Entered by the Standard Motor Company and driven by Bolton/Rothschild. This car retired with a faulty radiator during the fourth hour. It had been in 28th place the hour before.

Lotus Elite, No.41. GT Category. Chassis No. 1016 P, engine No. 7533, registration WUU 2. Entered by Bill Frost and driven by Lumsden/Riley. This Lotus was placed eighth on distance after completing 2259.36 miles in 24 hours at an average speed of 94.14mph. In addition it won the 1500cc class.

MGA Twin Cam, No.33. GT category. Chassis No. YD3/627/5, engine No. 16G/U/306, registration SRX 210. Entered by Ted Lund and driven by Lund/Escott. This car was retired in the 21st hour and had been in fifteenth place the hour before.
MG No.33 had been stopped by the officials at the beginning of the race and then continued until the 21st hour when problems with the gearbox forced retirement.

Triumph TR3, No.25. GT category. Chassis No X 628, engine No X 711 E, registration XHP 939. Entered by the Standard Motor Company and driven by Jopp/Stoop. This TR3 retired with an overheated engine during the tenth hour but had been in eighteenth place the hour before. **Triumph TR3, No.27.** GT category. Chassis No X 627, engine No X 701 E, registration XHP 938. Entered by the Standard Motor Company and driven by Sanderson/Dubois. This car retired with a punctured radiator during the 23rd hour, having been in seventh place an hour earlier.

Lotus Fifteen, No.54. Sports category. Chassis No. 659, engine No. 441/2/2. Entered by Team Lotus and driven by Taylor/Sieff. This Lotus retired during the fifth hour and had been in 48th place the hour before.
This was not a brilliant race for the Lotus which had repeatedly stopped in the pits from the beginning and was finally brought to a halt by an ignition fault.

1960

There were 55 cars at the start of the 1960 24 Hour Race, and six of the first seven to finish were Ferraris. The Belgian team, Gendebien and Frère won the race by completing 2620.65 miles in their Ferrari TR60 at an average speed of 109.19mph. Second place was taken by the 18-year-old Mexican, Ricardo Rodriguez, in another Ferrari.

AC Ace Bristol, No.30. GT category. Chassis No. BEX 289, engine No. 100 D 627, registration VD 21156. Entered by Équipe Lausannoise and driven by Wicky/Gachnang. This Swiss entry finished the race but was not placed as it did not complete the minimum mileage.

Aston Martin, DBR1, No.7. Sports category. Chassis No. DBR 1/3, registration FSH 360. Entered by Border Reivers and driven by Salvadori/Clark. This Aston was placed third on distance after completing 2558.63 miles in 24 hours at an average speed of 106.61mph and was sixth in the Index of Performance.

At the start, Jim Clark was the first to leap into his car and set off up the long Dunlop curve. The magnificent success of this privately-entered ex-Works car – already this year it had won the Nürburgring 1000km and was in the limelight in the Tourist Trophy – was largely due to the brilliance of the two drivers who drove with great consistency during the quiet intervals and with great speed in the more heated ones. The maximum speed registered on the Mulsanne Straight was 149mph.

AC Ace Bristol, No.57. GT category. Chassis No. BEX 365, engine No. 100 D 708, registration 1445 ER 76. Entered by J. Rambaux and driven by Rambaux/Boutin. This car was retired during the fourteenth hour with a broken piston.

Aston Martin DBR1, No.8. Sports category. Chassis No. DBR 1/2. Entered by Major I. Baillie and driven by Baillie/Fairman. This Aston was placed ninth on distance after completing 2349.23 miles at an average speed of 97.88mph and fourth in the Sports category. Ferrari took all intervening five places between the Clark/Salvadori Aston No.7 which came third and the Baillie/Fairman car.

On Sunday afternoon, Jack Fairman became entrenched in the sand on the Mulsanne Curve and took almost an hour to extricate himself. This ex-Works Aston had won at Le Mans the previous year with Salvadori and Shelby.

Austin Healey 3000, No.23. GT category. Engine No. 29D/U/H7326. Entered by Jack Sears, and driven by Sears/Riley. Retired with big end failure during the tenth hour.

Jaguar, Type E2A, No.6. Sports category. Engine No. EE 1308/10. Entered by Briggs Cunningham and driven by Hansgen/Gurney. This car retired during the tenth hour and had been in 34th place the hour before.

Walt Hansgen showed great promise during practice on Wednesday and on the dry track, completed a lap in 4min 4.6sec; the best time. During the race his first stop came after only three laps with a fuel leak which took eight minutes to rectify. The car was then involved in a collision with a Ferrari from which it emerged virtually unscathed, which is more than can be said for the Ferrari. During the night a second crash, this time at Mulsanne and involving several cars, was indirectly responsible for this Jaguar's retirement. An injector pipe fractured and was replaced but after 85 laps a piston blew. This car's maximum speed on the Mulsanne Straight was 153mph.

Austin-Healey Sprite Sebring, No.46. Sports category. Chassis No. XSP 1548/1, registration No. 5983 AC. Entered by Donald Healey and driven by Dalton/Colgate Jnr. This Healey was placed twentieth on distance after completing 2055.15 miles in 24 hours at an average speed of 85.63mph, was eleventh in the Index of Performance and won the 851-1000cc class.

Jaguar D-type, No.5. Sports category. Chassis No. XKD 606, engine No. BB 8 648/8, registration RSF 301. Entered by Écurie Écosse and driven by Flockhart/Halford. This car retired during the fourteenth hour after completing 168 laps. The car's maximum speed at Les Hunaudières was 157mph and after the first two hours of racing in the pouring rain, Ron Flockhart was placed third overall. The car, a Le Mans veteran which had competed in the race four times and came second in 1957, maintained its position among the first few until 5.30am when it stopped at Arnage with a broken crankshaft.

Lotus Elite, No.41. GT category. Chassis No. 1027, registration FP98. Entered by Team Lotus and driven by Wagstaff/Marsh. This car was placed fourteenth on distance after completing 2146.78 miles in 24 hours at an average speed of 89.45mph. This Lotus came first in the Thermal Efficiency Cup which had started the year before, was twelfth in the Index of Performance, seventh in the GT category and came second in the 1300cc class, which was won by the only other Elite to finish, No.44. Its maximum speed on the Mulsanne was 123mph.
All the Works Lotus were fitted with Lotus Formula 1 type suspension.

Lotus Elite, No.42. GT category. Engine No. FWE 400/15/8211. Entered by Team Lotus and driven by Buxton/Allen. This Elite retired with clutch problems during the eighteenth hour and had been in 30th position the hour before.

Lotus Elite, No.43. GT category. Chassis No.1125, registration 373 NPF. Entered by G. Baillie and driven by Baillie/Parkes. The car retired during the seventeenth hour and had been in 25th position the hour before. This Lotus, notable for its fine performance through the Esses, finally came to a halt with failed transmission after numerous pit stops.

Lotus Elite, No.44. Category GT. Chassis No. 1246, registration 24 KC 75. Entered by Roger Masson and driven by Masson/Laurent. This car was placed thirteenth on distance after completing 2182.88 miles at an average speed of 90.95mph, was sixth in the GT category and won the 1300cc class. This French Lotus ran a very consistent race and beat all the Works Lotus.

Lotus Elite, No.62. GT category. Chassis No. 1266, engine No. FWE 400/15.8244. Entered by Team Lotus. This fifth Lotus, one of the reserve cars, was driven during practice, by Jonathan Sieff who left the track on the Mulsanne Straight and was seriously injured. The car itself was damaged beyond repair.

MGA, No.32. Sports category. Chassis No. YD3 627/S, registration SRX 210, twin cam engine. Entered by Ted Lund and driven by Lund/C. Escott. This car was placed twelfth on distance after completing 2188.70 miles in 24 hours at an average speed of 91.20mph. This valiant little MG which had already competed at Le Mans in 1959 won the 2-litre class.

Triumph TR4, No.28. Sports category. Engine No X 783, registration 926 HP. Entered by Standard-Triumph and driven by Ballisat/Becquart. This car finished the race but was disqualified as it had not achieved the minimum mileage. The three TR4s managed to arrive together at the finish, a feat which attracted the interest of the Press, even though none of the cars was placed.

Triumph TR4, No.59. Sports category, registration 928 HP. Entered by Standard-Triumph and driven by Leston/Rothschild. This car was not placed as it had completed an insufficient mileage. In the photograph the car is being driven by Les Leston, the well-known purveyor of car accessories. The maximum speed at Les Hunaudières was 127mph.

Triumph TR4, No.29. Sports category. Chassis No X 655, engine No X 784 E, registration 927 HP. Entered by Standard-Triumph and driven by Bolton/Sanderson. Like the other two Triumphs, this TR4 was not placed as it had completed an insufficient mileage. The sound of failing valve-gear was audible as the car was driven over the finishing line.

This was Ferrari's fifth victory in the Le Mans 24 Hour Race. Ph Hill and Gendebien set a new distance record by completing 2781.6 miles; their average speed was 115.90mph. Few manufacturers coul contest this supremacy. Of the British companies, Aston Martin alon was in with a chance, albeit slim; the rest of the British contingen was singularly lacking in sparkle.

AC Ace Bristol, No.28. GT category. Chassis No. BEX 1110, registration 966 HL 31. Entered by A. Chardonnet and driven by Magne/Alexandrovitch. The car was placed seventeenth on distance after completing 2179.32 miles in 24 hours at an average speed of 90.81mph.

This AC, entered by André Chardonnet, the French importer of the marque, won seventh place in the GT category.

AC Ace Bristol, No.29. GT category. Chassis No. BEX 399, registration VD 2065. Entered by Équipe Lausannoise and driven by Wicky/Berney. The car, which was in 32nd place the hour before, retired during the eleventh hour.

This Swiss AC was the first car to stop in the pits, although fortunately only briefly. According to contemporary sources the retirement, during the night, was due either to the engine's overheating or to problems with the clutch.

Aston Martin DB4 GT Zagato, No.1. GT category. Chassis No. 0180. Entered by J. Kerguen and driven by 'Franc' (Jacques Dewes) Kerguen. Retired in the 24th hour and had been ninth during the previous hour. After a superb race this white Aston pulled into the pits, but because of a flat battery failed to restart.

Aston Martin DB4 GT Zagato, No.3. GT category. Chassis No. 0183, registration 2 VEV. Entered by John Ogier and driven by Davison/Stillwell. This car retired during the third hour and had been in eighteenth place the hour before. Lack of coolant led to a blown head gasket which finished the race for this Australian-driven Zagato.

Aston Martin DB4 GT Zagato, No.2. GT category. Chassis No. 0182, registration 1 VEV. Entered by John Ogier and driven by Fairman/Consten. Retired during the 23rd hour and had been in 51st place the hour before. A blown gasket after 23 hours put an end to this Aston's race. Severe cooling problems plagued the Aston Zagatos which, it had been hoped, would prove a match for the Gran Tourismo Ferraris.

Aston Martin DBR1, No.4. Sports category. Chassis No. DBR 1/4, engine No. RB6/300/3. Entered by John Ogier and driven by Salvadori/Maggs. This Aston retired during the nineteenth hour and had been in fourth place the hour before. Unfortunately, an irreparable leak from the fuel tank finished the race for this aging Aston which had run a great race and kept up well with the leaders.

Aston Martin DBR1, No.5. Sports category. Chassis No. DBR 1/3, engine No. RB6/300/2, registration FSH 360. Entered by Border Reivers and driven by Flockhart/Clark. This car retired during the eleventh hour and had been in fifteenth place the hour before. Jim Clark left the start like a bullet from a gun and was under the Dunlop footbridge when the rest of the field had barely started. For the next ten hours, his driving was a virtuoso performance. At the beginning of the evening, the dark blue Aston had to stop in the pits and then during the night Clark was forced to halt at Arnage with clutch failure.

Austin-Healey 3000, No.21. GT category. Chassis No. HBN 10 339, registration DD 300. Entered by Écurie Chiltern and driven by Stoop/Bekaert. This Healey retired during the 23rd hour and had been in seventeenth position the hour before.
It had completed 254 laps and came close to finishing the race before retiring with engine and clutch failure.

Austin-Healey Sprite, No.42. Sports category. Chassis No. AN 547 399, registration 1411 WD. Entered by Donald Healey and driven by Colgate/Hawkins. It retired during the eighth hour and had been in 45th place the hour before. Just before midnight, valve problems finished the race for this Sprite.

Austin-Healey Sprite, No.46. Sports category. Chassis No. AN 547.402, registration 1413 WD. Entered by Écurie Écosse and driven by Sanderson/Mackay. This car, in 45th place the hour before, retired during the fifth hour when it rolled at the White House and the driver, Jim Mackay, was taken to hospital with a damaged spine.

Lotus Elite, No.41. GT category. Chassis No. 1448, registration 3 CGJ. Entered by Los Amigos and driven by Malle/Carnegie. This Elite was forced to retire during the tenth hour when it ran out of petrol.

Lotus Elite, No.38. GT category. Chassis No. 1610, engine No. FWE 400/30/9519. Entered by Lotus Engineering and driven by Allen/T. Taylor. This car was placed twelfth on distance after completing 2234.92 miles in 24 hours at an average speed of 93.12mph. This Elite won the 1300cc class, was fourth in the GT category and was placed thirteenth in the Index of Performance.

Lotus Elite, No.40. GT category. Chassis No. 1440, registration 118 LF 75. Entered by Ecurie Edger and driven by Kosselek/Massenez. Placed thirteenth on distance after completing 2231.09 miles in 24 hours at an average speed of 92.96mph. This Elite, which was fifth in the GT class, came a close second in the 1300cc class, hard on the heels of the works Lotus No.38 which finished with only a 3.72 mile lead. Ecurie Edger, based at 20 rue des Acacias in Paris had Edouard Germain at its head.

Lotus Elite, No.39. GT category. Engine No. FWE/400/30/9629. Entered by Lotus Engineering and driven by Wyllie/Hunt. This Lotus over-heated and retired during the twentieth hour after being in 30th place the hour before.

Lotus Elite, No.51. Sports category. Engine No. FWMC/441/2/112. Entered by UDT Laystall and driven by Allison/MacKee. Retired in the eleventh hour and had been in 35th place the hour before. UDT entered this Elite with a view to winning the Index of Performance and Thermal Efficiency Cup. Though this was a brave entry, the small FWM Coventry-Climax dohc engine did not have the stamina for Le Mans and gave up the ghost.

Lotus Elite, No.62. GT category. Chassis No. 1367, registration No. 4909 DT 78. Entered by M. Porthault and driven by Porthault/Devos. This car was a reserve and not allowed to start.

Austin-Healey 3000, No.61. GT category. Chassis No. RN4 22 881, registration TON 792. Entered by Cambridge Racing and driven by J.M. Clark/J. Taylor. This car was third reserve and did not take part in the race.

MGA, No.58. Sports category. Chassis No. YD3 627 F, registration SRX 210. Entered by Ted Lund and driven by Lund/Olthoff. This Twincam MG retired after only fifteen laps during the second hour with a run big end.

Triumph TR4/S, No.25. Sports category. Chassis No X 657, registration 929 HP. Entered by Standard-Triumph and driven by Becquart/Rothschild. This car was placed fifteenth on distance after completing 2189.87 miles in 24 hours and at an average speed of 91.25mph. There was a lot of smoke issuing from this Triumph which finished 22nd in the Index of Performance, tenth in the sports category and last of the Triumphs. Triumph won the team prize.

Triumph TR4/S, No.26. Sports category. Registration 927 HP. Entered by Standard-Triumph and driven by Leston/Slotemaker. This car was placed eleventh on distance after completing 2332.16 miles in 24 hours at an average speed of 97.17mph.

Triumph TR4/S, No.27. Sports category. Chassis No X 654, registration 926 HP. Entered by Standard-Triumph and driven by Bolton/Ballisat. Ninth on overall distance after completing 2373.23 miles in 24 hours at an average speed of 98.90mph.
This Triumph was placed seventh in the sports category and seventeenth in the Index of Performance. It was the most successful Triumph, all of which finished the race.

Once again Phil Hill and Gendebien swept to victory in a Ferrari, the firm's sixth victory at Le Mans. The distance completed was 2765.86 miles at an average speed of 115.25mph. There were seventeen British starters and only six of them finished. This year marked the return of Sunbeam to Le Mans after an absence of 36 years.

AC Ace Bristol, No.60. GT category. Chassis No. BEX 1192, registration 3129 LL 75. Entered by A. Chardonnet and driven by Magne/Martin. The car retired after five hours with clutch problems. This Ace was fitted with one of the famous Bristol engines, the last to be used at Le Mans. The AC Ace was in 35th position during the hour before it retired.

Aston Martin P212, No.11. Experimental category. Chassis No. DB 212/1. Entered by David Brown and driven by G. Hill/R. Ginther. The car retired during the seventh hour. This Aston treated the onlookers to the drama of a veritable clash of Titans. Brilliantly driven, it surprised all the sceptics by being the first under the Dunlop bridge ahead of the Ferrari prototypes and completed the first lap in first place. Alas, a pit stop to repair the dynamo took just a little too long and in his haste to catch up on lost time Graham Hill changed into third gear instead of fifth, bending a valve.

Aston Martin DB4 GT Zagato, No.12. GT category. Chassis No. 0193, registration 1571 TTA 75. Entered by J. Kerguen and driven by Kerguen/'Franc'. This Aston retired during the twelfth hour with a blown gasket; the car had been in twentieth place the hour before. Aston Zagatos were still suffering from cooling problems.

Aston Martin DB4 GT Zagato, No.14. GT category. Chassis No. 0200, registration 22 XKX. Entered by M. Salmon and driven by Salmon/Baillie. This Zagato retired when a piston broke at 1.27am during the twelfth hour. The car had been in 24th place the hour before.

Austin-Healey 3000, No.24. GT category. Chassis No. HBN/7/10339, registration DD 300. Entered by Ecurie Chiltern and driven by Olthoff/Whitmore. This car retired during the ninth hour and had been in tenth place the hour before.

Jaguar E-type, No.8. GT category. Chassis No. 86 0458, registration 503 BBO. Entered by M. Charles and driven by Charles/Coundley. This Jaguar retired during the fourth hour with engine failure.

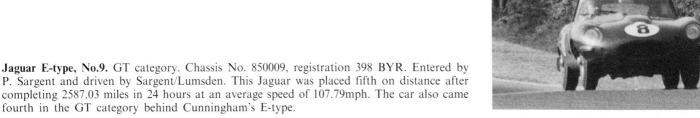

Jaguar E-type, No.9. GT category. Chassis No. 850009, registration 398 BYR. Entered by P. Sargent and driven by Sargent/Lumsden. This Jaguar was placed fifth on distance after completing 2587.03 miles in 24 hours at an average speed of 107.79mph. The car also came fourth in the GT category behind Cunningham's E-type.

Jaguar E-type, No.10. GT category. Chassis No. 860 630. Entered by Briggs Cunningham and driven by Cunningham/Salvadori. This car was placed fourth on distance after completing 2589.01 miles in 24 hours at an average speed of 107.88mph. This was the most successful of the E-types and finished third in its class in addition to coming third in the GT category after two Ferrari GTOs. Salvadori had driven the fastest lap (4min 16sec) during practice. At the finish the E-type was smoking a little – which was hardly surprising, perhaps.

Key to colour section: P97. Aston Martin No.3 in 1958. P98. *Above* Jaguar No.10 in 1962; *below* Jaguar No.9 in 1964. P99. *Above* Jaguar No.14 in 1964 (during trials in April); *below* Jaguar No.15 (during trials in April). P100. Aston Martin No.14 in 1956. P101. *Above* Aston Martin No.20 in 1957; *below* Aston Martin No.5 in 1959. P102. *Above* Lister-Jaguar No.9 in 1958; *below* Jaguars Nos.14 and 15 in 1963. P103. Two views of Jaguar No.1 as it stops to refuel in 1956. Bueb hands over to Hawthorn. P104. *Above* Aston Martin No.19 in 1963; *below* Aston Martin No.7 in 1963. P105. Aston Martin No.7 in 1960. P106. Aston Martin No.4 and Maserati No.1 in 1958. P107. *Above* Aston Martin No.4 in 1959 and *below* Aston Martin No.50 in 1979. P108. *Above* Lotus No.55 in 1957 and *below* Lotus No.42 in 1959. P109. *Above* Lotus No.44 in 1962 and *below* same car in 1967. P110. Austin-Healey No.42 in 1961 *above* and *below* Austin-Healey No.46 in 1961. P111. *Above* Austin-Healey No.21 in 1961 and *below* MG No.58. P112. *Above* Triumphs No.65 and No.50 in 1964, *below left* AC No.29 in 1959, *below right* Triumph No.27 in 1959. *Note. We are indebted to Jean Fondin for most of the colour photographs.*

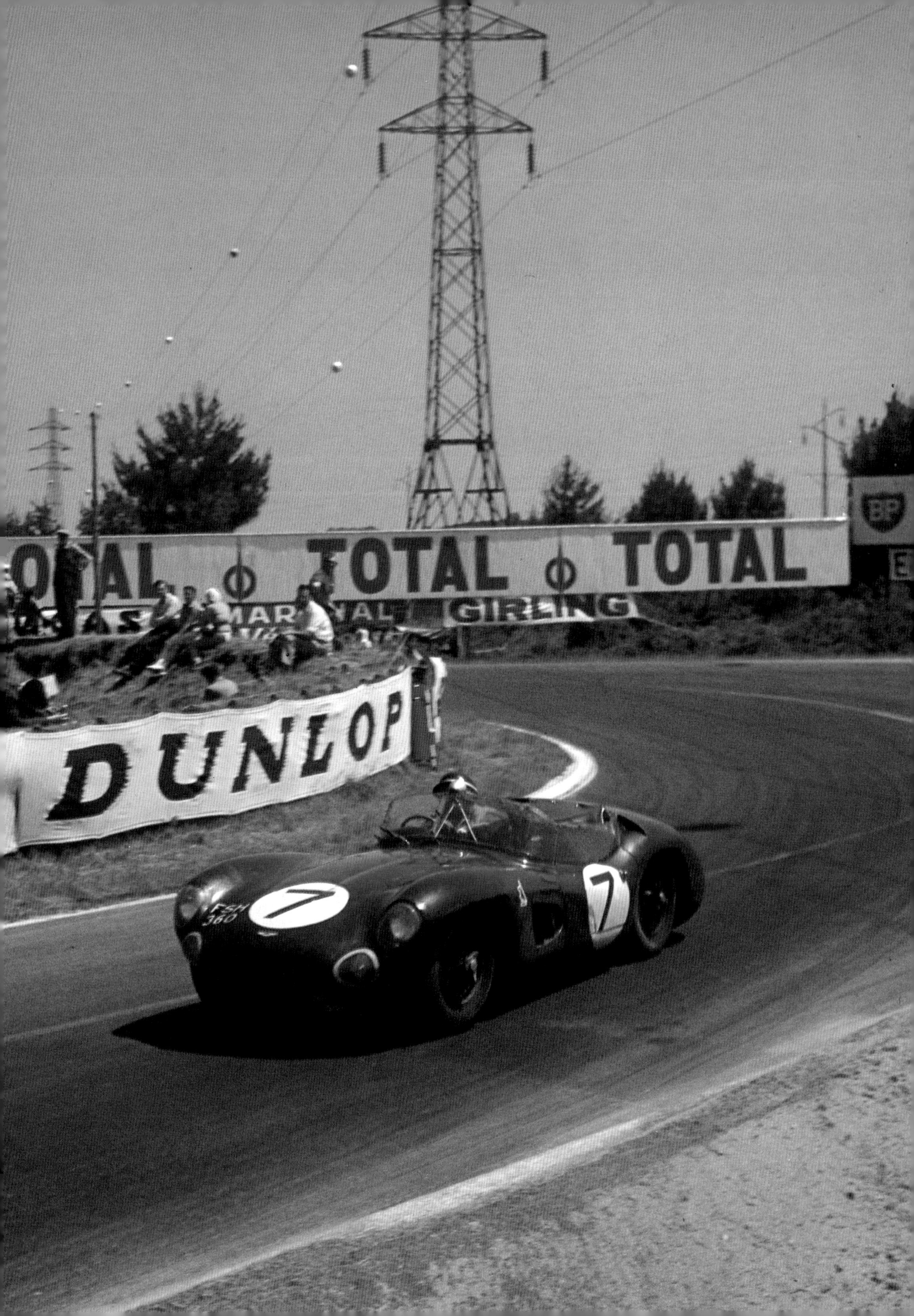
TOTAL
TOTAL
GIRLING
BP
DUNLOP
7
FSH
360
7

Lotus Elite, No.44. GT category. Chassis No. 1678, engine No. FWE 10/380. Entered by Lotus Engineering and driven by Hobbs/Gardner. Placed eighth on distance after completing 2390.46 miles in 24 hours at an average speed of 99.60mph. This Lotus Elite won the 1300cc class – the third year running that the class had been won by an Elite. It also took first place in the Index of Thermal Efficiency and was third in the Index of Performance and sixth in the GT category thus cocking a splendid snook at the officials of the ACO.

Lotus Elite, No.45. GT category. Chassis No. 1792, engine No. FWE 10 381. Entered by Lotus Engineering and driven by Hunt/Wyllie. This car was placed eleventh on distance after completing 2319.86 miles in 24 hours at an average speed of 96.66mph.

Lotus Twentythree, No.47. Prototype category. Ford Cosworth 105E 997cc engine, No. S 213259 E. Chassis No. K 23 AZ entered by Lotus Engineering and driven by Clark/T. Taylor. Two of these redoubtable Lotus Twentythrees were presented for weighing in and were sent away as the ground clearance was insufficient. After correcting that, they were sent away a second time because the wheels were fixed with four bolts in front and six at the rear. In order to conform, wheels with four bolts were flown specially from England only to be refused by the authorities who considered that four bolts were insufficient on safety grounds. As a result, the authorities were accused of penalising Lotus in the hope that this would improve France's chances in the Index of Performance.

Lotus Twentythree, No.48. Prototype category. Entered by UDT- Laystall. This car, fitted with a 750cc engine, was also turned away by the technical committee and did not compete in the race. The final assertion by the ACO was that the Lotus Twentythrees were not 'in the spirit of Le Mans.' Colin Chapman was understandably furious as his cars were regularly checked by the FIA and his treatment by the ACO officials resulted in a long-held grudge against the race.

1963

The seventh Le Mans victory for Ferrari, won this time by Scarfiotti and Bandini. The two Italians beat the distance record by completing 2834.51 miles at an average speed of 118.11mph. With six of their cars occupying the first six places, Ferrari had swept the board. The first British car to finish, E-type Jaguar No.15, was placed ninth.

Aston Martin DB4 GT, No.8. GT category. Chassis No. 0195. Entered by Aston Martin Lagonda and driven by McLaren/Ireland. This car retired during the sixth hour. Bruce McLaren was driving when the car's engine quite literally exploded at the end of the Mulsanne straight. The car was immediately enveloped in a cloud of smoke from the fourteen litres of oil instantly ejected. This incident was to lead to the tragic death of Bino Heins who had been driving an Alpine and to accidents to Salvadori's Jaguar, Manzon's RB and Kerguen's Aston.

Aston Martin DB4 GT, No.7. GT category. Chassis No. 0194. Entered by Aston Martin Lagonda and driven by Schlesser/Kimberley. Retired with engine failure during the eleventh hour and had been in third place the hour before. This Aston ran a superb race and led the GT category for a time.

Aston Martin P215, No.18. Prototype category. Chassis No. DP 215. Entered by David Brown and driven by P. Hill/Bianchi. The car was retired during the fourth hour and had been in 37th place the hour before. This new prototype, based on the P212 which raced at Le Mans the year before, retired after only three hours with transmission problems.

Aston Martin DB4 GT Zagato, No.19. GT category. Chassis No. 0193, registration 1571 TTA 75. Entered by J. Kerguen and driven by 'Franc'/Kerguen. This Aston retired during the seventh hour and had been in 23rd place an hour before. 'Franc' (Jacques Dewes) was driving when he became involved in the mêlée caused by Aston Martin No.8 at Les Hunaudières. He had been travelling at about 155mph and was lucky to escape unscathed, but the transaxle was too badly damaged for him to finish the race.

Austin-Healey Sprite, No.42. Prototype category. Chassis No. HAN 763/H 73. 14, registration 58 FAC. Entered by Donald Healey and driven by Whitmore/Olthoff. This car retired during the ninth hour and had been in nineteenth place the hour before. Austin-Healey had their sights on the Index of Performance when they entered this 95bhp Sprite; unfortunately, it went off the track at the White House.

Jaguar E-type, No.14. GT category. Chassis No. S 850 664, registration 5114 WK. Entered by Briggs Cunningham and driven by Hansgen/Pabst. This extremely fast 300bhp Jaguar with lightweight aluminium body retired during the first hour due to a failed gearbox.

Jaguar E-type, No.15. GT category. Chassis No. S 580 659. Entered by Briggs Cunningham and driven by Richards/Grossmann. This Jaguar finished in ninth place on distance after completing 2372.45 miles in 24 hours at an average speed of 98.85mph. The American team was delayed in the pits for almost two hours, first with gearbox problems and then when the brake pedal pivot pin worked loose resulting in brake failure and the inadvertent redesigning of the front end of the car as it left the track. All this did not prevent the duo acquitting themselves well; they won the 4-litre class, and were eleventh in the Index of Performance and fifteenth in the Thermal Efficiency Cup with a fuel consumption of 10.21mpg.

Jaguar E-type, No.16. GT category. Registration 5116 WK. Entered by Briggs Cunningham and driven by Salvadori/Cunningham. This E-type retired during the sixth hour and had been in 37th place the hour before. Salvadori was about 20 yards behind McLaren's Aston when the Aston's engine exploded on the Mulsanne straight spraying oil on to the track. Salvadori, seeing what had happened, braked so hard that the car was thrown off balance and turned over. Salvadori himself, was thrown out of his car but picked himself up with only bruises. Bino Heins, who was driving an Alpine, was also involved in this multiple accident; he was less lucky and lost his life.

Lister-Jaguar, No.17. Prototype category. Engine No. R 1035/9, registration WTM 446. Entered by Peter Sargent and driven by Sargent/Lumsden. This Lister-Jaguar, the last to be raced at Le Mans, retired after only three hours when it got stuck in the sand at the Mulsanne corner completely destroying a wing. The car, which had a 300bhp E-type engine, had been in 21st, 16th and 38th places respectively at the end of each of its three hours of racing. Towards the end of those hours it was suffering problems with the transmission which contributed to the decision to retire.

MGB, No.31. GT category. Chassis No. CHN 3/3699, registration 7 DBL. Entered by Alan Hutcheson and driven by Hopkirk/Hutcheson. This MGB finished in twelfth place overall after completing 2207.14 miles at an average speed of 91.96mph, was second in the 2-litre class and eighth in Thermal Efficiency with a fuel consumption of 13.12mpg. Paddy Hopkirk got stuck in the sand which slowed the car down considerably and damaged the clutch during extrication. Despite all this, this was a very successful race for the little MG.

Lotus Elite, No.39. GT category. Chassis No. 1678. Entered by Team Elite and driven by Wagstaff/Fergusson. This Elite was placed tenth on distance after completing 2256.94 miles in 24 hours at an average speed of 94.05mph. This highly successful partnership won the GT category for cars under 2-litres, the 1300cc class, was third in the Thermal Efficiency Index (20.71mpg) and ninth in the Index of Performance. Pat Fergusson got stuck in the sand twice in a row at Mulsanne.

Lotus Elite, No.38. GT category. Chassis No. 1792. Entered by Team Elite and driven by Gardner/Coundley. This car retired during the sixteenth hour and had been in thirteenth place the hour before. Electrical problems followed by engine failure put this strong runner out of the race.

1964

Ferrari won the Le Mans 24 Hours race for the eighth time with a 275P driven by Guichet and Vaccarella which beat the distance record by completing 2917.53 miles at an average speed of 121.56mph. Average speeds were inexorably creeping up towards 125mph. Twenty-four competitors finished, four of them driving British cars.

Aston Martin DB4 GT, No.18. GT category. Chassis No. 0370, engine No. 1288/0. Entered by Mike Salmon and driven by Salmon/Sutcliffe. This car, the only Aston in the race, was disqualified during the nineteenth hour for making an unscheduled stop for more oil. The car had been running a good race and had been in eleventh place the hour before it was disqualified.

Austin-Healey Sprite, No.53. Prototype category. Chassis No. XSP 2173. Entered by the Donald Healey Motor Company and driven by Baker/Bradley. This car was placed 24th on distance after completing 2148.91 miles in 24 hours at an average speed of 89.54mph. This little Sprite was placed last in the Index of Performance and was also the last car to finish this very long race. During the final hour, the car made a long pit stop but unexpectedly set off again to the delighted cheers of the crowd.

Jaguar Lightweight E-type, No.16. GT category. Chassis No. RA 1347-95. Entered by Peter Lindner Racing and driven by Lindner/Nocker; this car retired during the sixteenth hour and had been in 29th position the hour before.

Despite Lindner's numerous improvements, this German-entered car was showing its age and its entry had not posed much of a threat to the GT class. From dawn the car had been plagued with cooling problems and finally gave up the ghost with a blown gasket. A few months later, Peter Lindner lost his life driving the same car in the 1000km de Paris. Franco Patria and three course officials also died in the accident.

Jaguar Lightweight E-type, No.17. GT category. Chassis No. RAI 34 895. Entered by Peter J. Sargent and driven by Lumsden/Sargent. This car retired during the eighth hour with gearbox failure; it had been in 34th place the hour before. The Jaguar was placed twelfth during the fifth hour which was its best position.

Lotus Elan, No.38. Prototype category. Chassis No. LM 156, registration 77 QH 75. Entered by Royal Élysées and driven by Gelée/Richard. This car retired during the third hour and had been in 44th place the hour before. An overheated engine finished the race for this blue and yellow Lotus Elan entered by the French importer. This was the only Lotus Elan to race at Le Mans; Ian Walker had hoped to compete with his in this race but it was damaged at the Nürburging.

Lotus Elite, No.43. GT category. Chassis No. 41-10391, registration FWE 400. Entered by Team Elite and driven by Hunt/Wagstaff. Placed 22nd on distance after completing 2222.70 miles in 24 hours at an average speed of 92.61mph. This was the last Lotus Elite to race at Le Mans and it left on a high note by winning the 1300cc class and was eighteenth in the Index of Performance. The distance completed in 1964 was actually 35 miles less than in 1963.

MGB, No.37. GT category. Chassis No. ADO 23/986, registration BMO 541 B. Entered by the British Motor Corporation and driven by Hopkirk/Hedges. Placed nineteenth on distance after completing 2398.70 miles at an average speed of 99.95mph.

This car was also seventeenth in the Index of Performance, sixth in the GT class for its capacity and Paddy Hopkirk added 186 miles to his 1963 total. The team also won *Motor*'s prize for the highest placed British entry.

Triumph Spitfire, No.49. Prototype category. Chassis No. X985. Entered by Standard-Triumph International and driven by Tullius/Rothschild. This car retired during the third hour and had been in 45th position the hour before.

Michael Rothschild departed from the track on the Dunlop bend, supposedly unbalanced by the whistle of a powerful Ford, and hit the barriers on both sides before coming to a halt. He was just missed by Rodriguez in a Ferrari. Rothschild was taken to hospital with mild shock. Bob Tullius went on to take Jaguar to Le Mans twenty years later.

Triumph Spitfire, No.50. Prototype category. Entered by Standard-Triumph International and driven by Hobbs/Slotemaker. Placed 21st on distance after completing 2273.48 miles in 24 hours at an average speed of 94.72mph. This was the only Triumph Spitfire to finish and was sixteenth in the Index of Performance and third in the GT 1001-1150cc class. The car was clocked at 135.46mph on the Mulsanne Straight.

Triumph Spitfire, No.65. Prototype category. Chassis No X 937. Entered by Standard-Triumph International and driven by Piot/Marnat. This Triumph retired during the fourteenth hour and had been in 28th place an hour before.

Whilst braking at Tertre Rouge, Marnat's foot slipped off the pedal and the car went off the track. After an inspection in the pits it was clear that the steering was bent and the rear of the car damaged. Three-quarters of an hour later, overcome by the exhaust fumes from his own car, Marnat lost control again, this time in front of the refuelling area. The car went through the barriers on the off-side of the Dunlop Curve which had been an unlucky part of the course for Triumph. Marnat was taken to hospital with serious injuries.

1965

1965 saw the ninth and last victory at Le Mans for a Ferrari. Gregory and Rindt, privately entered by Luigi Chinetti's NART (North American Racing Team), ran a brilliant race completing 2906.22 miles at an average speed of 121.09mph.
The Rover-BRM gas turbine car was tenth and the highest placed British car.

Austin-Healey Sprite, No.48. Prototype category. Chassis No. HAN 8/R65/135, registration ENX 416 C. Entered by Donald Healey and driven by Aaltonen/Baker. This car retired during the 22nd hour and was in fourteenth place the hour before. Great things were expected of this prototype which was fitted with a 1300cc Cooper 'S' engine; so, too, was much expected of the car's famous Scandinavian driver. Early in the race, however, Baker lost a rear brake caliper and became involved in a rear-end shunt. Then, later on, the car was retired after a series of transmission problems leaving Healey's other Sprite prototype to take the glory.

Austin-Healey Sprite, No.49. Prototype category. Chassis No. HAN 8/R65/52, registration ENX 415 C. Entered by Donald Healey and driven by Hawkins/Rhodes. This car was placed twelfth on distance after completing 2315.50 miles in 24 hours at an average speed of 96.48mph.
Despite problems with the front brake discs, this Sprite was seventh in the Index of Performance, third in the Thermal Efficiency Index (19.035mpg) and won the 1300cc class. The car arrived at Le Mans painted in fluorescent colours, but this had to be changed to green on the orders of the race officials.

Triumph Spitfire, No.52. GT category. Chassis No. FC 54 950, registration ADU 1B. Entered by Standard-Triumph and driven by Hobbs/Slotemaker. This car retired during the seventh hour and was in 32nd place the hour before. At the beginning of the night, the Dutchman, Rob Slotemaker was overtaken at the White House; he dipped his headlamps but did not return them to full beam in time to see the bend and crashed into the barriers. Although Slotemaker himself was unharmed the car suffered severe damage and could not be moved.

Triumph Spitfire, No.53. GT category. Engine No. FC 54 805 HE. Entered by Standard-Triumph and driven by Bradley/Bolton. This Triumph retired in the first hour after only nine laps with a damaged big end bearing. During practice, the car had completed a lap in 4min 56.1sec.

The Triumphs were entered in the GT class because of their standard gearboxes.

Triumph Spitfire, No.54. GT category. Engine No. FC 54 806 HE. Entered by Standard-Triumph and driven by Dubois/Piot. This car was placed fourteenth on distance after completing 2190.75 miles at an average speed of 91.28mph, thirteenth in the Index of Performance and second in the 1150cc class. This car, the 'Tail-end Charlie', was the last of a very small number of competitors to finish the 1965 event.

Triumph Spitfire, No.60. GT category. Chassis No. FC 545 953, registration ADU 4B. Entered by Standard-Triumph and driven by Thuner/Lampinen. This Triumph was placed thirteenth on distance after completing 2282.77 miles in 24 hours at an average speed of 95.12mph.
It won the 1150cc class and finished best of the four Triumphs entered.

MGB, No.39. GT category. Chassis No. GHN 3/59H27, registration DRX 2556. Entered by the British Motor Corporation and driven by Hopkirk/Hedges. This car was placed eleventh on distance after completing 2357.95 miles in 24 hours at an average speed of 98.25mph. The fuel consumption was 13.248mpg. The MGB was by now an old hand at Le Mans always running a consistent race, driven by excellent drivers and troubled by only minor problems.

1966

From 1966, America took over from Ferrari and won a series of Le Mans victories. The McLaren/Amon Ford smashed the previous distance record by completing 3009.36 miles and easily broke the 200km/h (125mph) barrier with an average speed of 130.98mph. The Ford GT40s owed everything to Britain (where they were designed and manufactured) but were nonetheless considered an all-American success.

Austin-Healey Sprite No.48. Prototype category. Chassis No. HAN 8R 144, engine No. XSP 26043, registration HNX 456D. Entered by Donald Healey and driven by Rhodes/Baker. This Sprite retired during the sixteenth hour with an oil leak.

Austin-Healey Sprite, No.49. Prototype category. Chassis No. HAN 8R 143, engine No. XSP 26044, registration HNX 455D. Entered by Donald Healey and driven by Hopkirk/Hedges. This car retired during the twenty-first hour and had been in sixteenth place the hour before. Oil leaks caused both Austin Healey prototypes to retire. The capacity of these cars was 79 litres of fuel, 13 litres of Castrol oil and 13 litres of coolant.

1967

This was an intelligently run race and was won again by the Americans. Gurney and Foyt smashed the distance record and exceeded 5000km for the first time, completing 3251.572 miles in 24 hours at an average speed of 135.48mph. The British entry was extremely slim but Austin-Healey managed to finish creditably.

Lotus 47 Europa, No.44. Prototype category. Driven by Wagstaff/Preston, it retired during the fifth hour. Brake problems and a blown head gasket put an end to the race for the only Europa to be raced at Le Mans. This was also the last car to be entered by Lotus in the 24 hour race.

Austin-Healey Sprite, No.51. Prototype category. Driven by Baker/Hedges. This car was placed fifteenth on distance after completing 2421.51 miles in 24 hours at an average speed of 100.90mph, thirteenth in the Index of Performance and eleventh in the prototype category. The car finished the race with its back end redesigned after a tail-end collision caused by a brake seizing when going through the Esses. Apart from this incident the Baker/Hedges Sprite ran a very consistent race with a fuel consumption of 18.835mpg.

1968

This year saw another Ford victory in this race where one win is often followed by further success. No records were beaten by the victors, Lucien Bianchi and Pedro Rodriguez, who completed 2766.89 miles at an average speed of 115.29mph. For political reasons, (this was the year of the student riots) the race was run in September.

Austin-Healey Sprite, No.50. Sports Prototype category. Driven by Enever/Poole. This car was placed fifteenth on distance after completing 2125.75 miles in 24 hours at an average speed of 94.73mph. This little Sprite which developed only 111bhp and weighed 1474lb ran a superb race. The car was tenth in the Index of Performance, eleventh in the sports prototype category and was the last car to finish.

Healey, No.47. Sports Prototype category. Driven by Hedges/Baker and retired during the third hour. This unique Healey developed only 245bhp from its Coventry Climax engine and really did not have enough power. But it was clutch failure that was the cause of retirement.

1969

Healey, No.37. Sports Prototype category. Driven by Baker/Harris, it retired during the fourth hour. The Healey's radiator was pierced by a piece of wreckage left on the track after an accident in the first lap and a gasket finally blew.

This was the first Le Mans victory for a young lad who was to make a career there – Jacky Ickx. Driving with Oliver in a Ford GT40 he came close to breaking the 5000km barrier by completing 3105.612 miles (4998km), which he did at an average speed of 129.400mph. There were only four British cars at the start; Healey Chevron, Lola and Nomad; none of them finished. This was the only occasion on which Nomad took part in a Le Mans race.

1970

Healey, No.34. Sports Prototype category. Entered by Donald Healey Motors and driven by Enever/Hedges. This Healey retired in the penultimate hour of the race with engine failure.

Porsche won the first of a long line of Le Mans victories. In addition to an overall win with a distance of 2863.16 miles at a slightly reduced average speed of 119.30mph, Hermann and Attwood won the Sports category and the 5-litre class. Again, British participation in the race was slim with only Lola, Healey and Chevron starting.

1977

1977 witnessed a fourth Porsche victory by Jacky Ickx, Barth and Haywood driving a 936. They completed 2902.82 miles at an average speed of 120.95mph. Aston Martin made a comeback to Le Mans after an absence of twelve years.

Aston Martin AMV8, No.83. GT Prototype category. Entered by Robin Hamilton and driven by Hamilton/Preece/Salmon. This car finished seventeenth on distance after completing 2203.68 miles at an average speed of 91.20mph, was third in the GT Prototype category and won the 5-litre class. This powerful Aston developed 520-530bhp and was entered by the Aston Martin dealer and enthusiast Robin Hamilton, thus renewing the tradition of Aston Martin at Le Mans. The car was slowed down by brake problems resulting in a change of discs. However, it finished within 82 laps of the winner (Porsche) and ran an excellent race. This was one of the reserve cars and raced as the result of a last-minute withdrawal.

1979

This was Porsche's fifth victory at Le Mans though, perhaps, not one of its most brilliant. Ludwig and the Whittington brothers completed 2593.56 miles at an average speed of 108.06mph, improving only slightly on Hawthorn and Bueb's achievement in 1955. Two Chevrons and three Lolas were entered in this race.

Aston Martin AMV8, No.5. GT Prototype category. Entered by Robin Hamilton and driven by Hamilton/Preece/Salmon. This Aston retired at 5.15pm at *poste 125*. An oil leak discovered at the first refuelling was responsible. Robin Hamilton drove for almost the whole $3\frac{1}{4}$ hours.

1982

This was Porsche's seventh victory at Le Mans and the sixth for Ickx, partnered this time by the Englishman Derek Bell who won with Ickx in 1975. They completed 3044.15 miles in their 956T at an average speed of 126.84mph. Le Mans was open to Group C cars for the first time in 1982 and saw the arrival of the Aston Martin Nimrod.

Aston Martin Nimrod, No.31. NRAC 2/3 Group C. Entered by Nimrod Racing Automobiles and driven by Evans/Lees/Needell, this car retired during the fourth hour after Needell left the road on the Mulsanne Straight as a result of a burst tyre or failed suspension.

Aston Martin Nimrod, No.32. Group C. Entered by Viscount Downe/Pace Petroleum and driven by Mallock/Salmon/Phillips. This Nimrod was placed seventh on distance after completing 2684.93 miles at an average speed of 111.87mph. Robin Hamilton, the Aston Martin dealer and enthusiast, who had reintroduced Aston Martins to Le Mans in 1977 was the force behind the new Nimrods. The Nimrod-AM chassis was based on the Lola T70 and as a result the car was rather heavy. In spite of that the Nimrods certainly gave the Group C class something to worry about and No.32 took fourth place on distance in the Group C class.

1983

1983 was a year of overwhelming success for Porsche; nine of their cars being in the first ten places. The victor's laurels went to Holbert, Haywood and Schuppan in a 956 with Ickx and Bell in second place. The winners had completed 3136.64 miles at an average speed of 130.69mph.

Aston Martin Nimrod, No.39. Group C2. Entered by Viscount Downe/Pace Petroleum and driven by Mallock/Salmon/Earle. This Nimrod retired after seventeen hours and thirteen minutes of racing. The car's fastest practice lap had been in 3min 35.$\frac{7}{8}$sec which made it sixteenth fastest after the Porsches and Lancias.

It was clocked at 160mph (258km/h) on Saturday afternoon as it went past the grandstands.

Aston Martin Emka, No.41. Entered by Emka Productions Ltd and driven by O'Rourke/Faure/Needell. This car was placed seventeenth on distance after completing 2328.82 miles in 24 hours at an average speed of 97.04mph. The Emka Aston Martin was clocked at 159mph on Saturday afternoon as it went past the grandstands.

1984

1984 marked the great comeback of Jaguar to Le Mans and the hundreds of supporters who had come to cheer on the Big Cat gave the race a carnival atmosphere. However, Porsche took its ninth victory with Pescarolo and Ludwig completing 3044.89 miles at an average speed of 126.87mph.

Nimrod C2B, No.31. Group C. Chassis No. 004. Entered by Viscount Downe/Aston Martin Lagonda and driven by Mallock/Olson. The car retired at the beginning of the night. Despite this very fast car's poor starting position, fifth row in the grid, it began to gain on the opposition and was fourteenth at 5pm and ninth at 7pm. By 8pm the Nimrod was in sixth place and posing a serious threat to the leaders, Porsche and Lancia. Everything seemed to be running smoothly until two tyres blew and the car returned to the pits. Prior to this the average lap time had been 3min 47sec.

At 9.30pm, tragedy struck. Drake Olson, who had taken over from his partner after an accident, went through the barriers at Ferme de Mulsanne killing one track official, Jacky Loiseau, and injuring another. Olson was taken to hospital in a state of shock.

Nimrod C2B, No.32. Group C. Entered by Viscount Downe/Aston Martin Lagonda and driven by Salmon/Sheldon/Attwood. This car retired at the beginning of the night.

At 9.23pm, half an hour after the incident when Nimrod No.31's tyres blew, this car crashed into the rails and caught fire, undoubtedly as a result of a blow-out. The driver, 37-year-old John Sheldon, was flown by helicopter to the Trousseau Hospital at Tours with serious burns. The race was stopped for more than an hour (from 9.25pm to 10.27pm) in order to clear the course. This Nimrod developed 560bhp and its stablemate, No.31, developed 585bhp.

Jaguar XJR-5, No.40. Group IMSA-GTP. Chassis No. 008. Entered by Group 44/Jaguar Cars and driven by Ballot Léna/Watson/Adamowicz. This Jaguar retired at 12.08pm. The car stopped in the pits at 11.20pm to tighten the left-hand rear suspension arm and then later, Adamowicz left the road at 5.33am at Tertre Rouge but was able to set off again shortly after midday. This Jaguar finally retired with a failed gearbox but won itself a huge round of applause from the crowd. It had been clocked at 212mph on the Mulsanne Straight on Saturday.

After an absence of twenty years the crowd's loud appreciation of Jaguar's efforts showed that the showmanship and success of former years had not been forgotten. Moreover, the public acclaim reflected the desire to see Jaguar, the outsider, pose a serious threat to the Porsche domination. The cars were built for Group 44 in Winchester, Virginia and designed by Lee Dykstra to run in the IMSA GTP races from 1982. In a season and a half they had already won five races.

Jaguar XJR-5, No.44. Group IMSA-GTP. Chassis No. 006. Entered by Group 44/Jaguar and driven by Redman/Tullius/Bundy. This Jaguar retired at 12.26pm, though before doing so it not only showed the seriousness of Jaguar's intent but was actually in the lead for a lap. Unfortunately, like its stablemate, this car had problems with the gearbox and had to stop at 7.09am to change the third-gear pinion. Retirement came after twenty hours and 26 minutes of racing; the car had completed 291 laps and 2463.736 miles. This 600bhp Jaguar was clocked at 216mph on the Mulsanne Straight on Saturday.

135

1985

Ludwig, Barilla and Winter beat all the records in their Porsche 956 by completing 3161.85 miles at an average speed of 131.74mph and Porsche won the Le Mans 24 Hours for the tenth time. Meanwhile Jaguar continued to prepare the ground for triumphs to come.

Aston Martin Cheetah, No.24. Group C2. Chassis No. 604-01. Entered by Cheetah Switzerland and driven by de Dryver/Bourgoignie/Cooper.
This car retired at 7.52pm when the offside rear wheel was severed near *Poste 96*.

Aston Martin Emka, No.66. Group C1. Entered by Emka Productions and driven by Needell/O'Rourke/Faure. This car was placed eleventh overall after completing 2859.63 miles in 24 hours at an average speed of 119.15mph. This was a fine performance despite a 43-minute stop on Saturday morning.

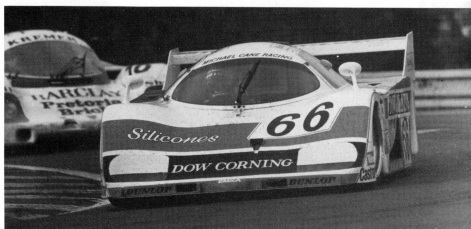

Jaguar XJR-5, No.40. Group GTP. Chassis No. 006. Entered by Group 44 and driven by Redman/Haywood/Adams. This car retired at 2.50am when it broke a nearside universal joint near *Poste 3*.

Jaguar XJR-5, No.44. Group GTP. Chassis No. 008. Entered by Group 44 and driven by Tullius/Robinson. This Jaguar was thirteenth overall after completing 2736.00 miles at an average speed of 114.00mph.
After a minor halt to change a 'black box', this Jaguar ran a consistent race and won the GTP class.

1986

This was Porsche's eleventh victory at Le Mans, won by Derek Bell accompanied this time by Stuck and Holbert. The winning distance was 3089.91 miles at an average speed of 128.75mph. There were nine Porsches in the first ten places.

Jaguar XJR-6, No.51. Chassis No. 8602. Entered by Silk Cut Racing and driven by Warwick/Cheever/Schlesser.
This Jaguar retired when a tyre blew on the Mulsanne Straight on Sunday morning. Schlesser, who was driving, managed to keep the car on the track but sadly a lot of damage had been done. The retirement was all the more galling as this car had moved into second place.

Jaguar XJR-6, No.52. Chassis No. 8601. Entered by Silk Cut Racing and driven by Redman/Haywood/Heyer. This car retired when it ran out of fuel at *Poste 83* at 9.52pm; it had been holding fifth and sixth places. Like No.51, this Jaguar had been clocked at 221mph at Les Hunaudières.

Jaguar XJR-6, No.53. Chassis No. 8603. Entered by Silk Cut Racing and driven by Percy/Brancatelli/Haywood. This car retired at 1.47am when the transmission failed. It was timed at 219mph at Les Hunaudières, a little slower than its stablemates.

1987

This was Porsche's seventh successive Le Mans victory, the twelfth in all. As in 1986, Stuck, Bell and Holbert were driving; their 962C completed 2977.471 miles at an average speed of 124.06mph. Derek Bell had now won Le Mans five times.

Jaguar XJR-8 LM, No.4. Entered by Silk Cut Racing and driven by Cheever/Boesel/Lammers. Despite some problems – with the gearbox (which had to be changed), a recalcitrant wheelhub and the throttle linkage – this Jaguar finished strongly. It completed 324 laps, 2730.91 miles at an average speed of 113.79mph.

Jaguar XJR-8 LM, No.5. Entered by Silk Cut Racing and driven by Watson/Lammers/Percy. This car retired, at 2.46am, when the rear offside tyre blew and the car rolled several times on the approach to the Mulsanne curve. Percy had just taken over the driving and had completed only four laps.

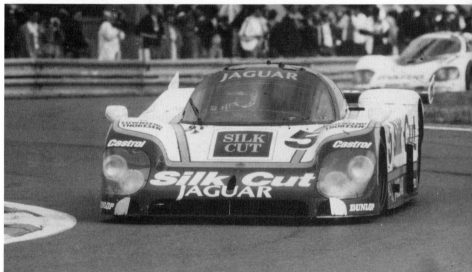

Jaguar XJR-8 LM, No.6. Entered by Silk Cut Racing and driven by Nielsen/Brundel/Hahne. This Jaguar was in second place when it retired at 7.47am with a blown head gasket. It was the best of the three Jaguars and had held the lead for three hours. Fuel consumption per lap for this car was 1.17gal (5.35l). It was clocked at 217mph on the Mulsanne Straight and at 156mph at the end of the grandstands.

1988

By 1988, Le Mans-goers had become seriously jaded by interminable Porsche victories; twelve in all. It was now that Jaguar, who had returned to Le Mans four years earlier after an absence of twenty years, swept to victory in a race that remade Jaguar's reputation.

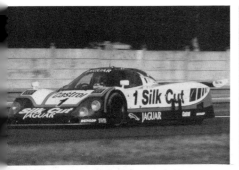 

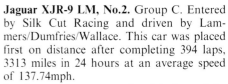

Jaguar XJR-9 LM, No.1. Group C. Entered by Silk Cut Racing and driven by Brundle/Nielsen, it retired during the nineteenth hour.

Jaguar XJR-9 LM, No.2. Group C. Entered by Silk Cut Racing and driven by Lammers/Dumfries/Wallace. This car was placed first on distance after completing 394 laps, 3313 miles in 24 hours at an average speed of 137.74mph.
So, Jaguar was once again victorious at Le Mans where the Coventry firm had made its reputation. After a gap of thirty-one years, Jaguar now celebrated its sixth win on the Sarthe circuit.
This was Jaguar's fourth victory in five races, in the FIA Championships.

Jaguar XJR-9 LM, No.3. Group C. Entered by Silk Cut Racing and driven by Watson/Boesel/Pescarolo, it retired during the eighth hour.

Jaguar XJR-9 LM, No.21. Group C. Entered by Silk Cut Racing and driven by Sullivan/Jones/Cobb. This Jaguar was placed sixteenth on distance after completing 331 laps in 24 hours.

Jaguar XJR-8 LM, No.22. Group C. Entered by Silk Cut Racing and driven by Daly/Cogan/Perkins.
This XJR-8 was placed fourth on distance after completing 383 laps in 24 hours at an average speed of 133.89mph and finished within eleven laps of the winner.

1989

The new Mercedes team had bet themselves that they would win the Le Mans 24 Hours at their first attempt; and they did just that. Better still they pulled off a resounding 1-2 to equal their 1952 achievement. Mass, Reuter and Dickens completed 3271.59 miles at an average speed of 136.70mph.

Aston Martin AMR1, No.18. Group C1. Entered by Aston Martin Lagonda and driven by Redman/Roe/Los. This car was placed eleventh on distance after completing 2859.49 miles in 24 hours at an average speed of 119.08mph.
Apart from some trouble with the exhaust, the first part of the race ran smoothly. Then at 1pm, Brian Redman was signalled to slow down on the Mulsanne and he returned to the pits with damage to the nearside rear suspension. Fortunately, he was able to set off again and was more than creditably placed.

Aston Martin AMR1, No.19. Group C1. Entered by Aston Martin and driven by Leslie/Mallock/Sears.
The race began badly for Leslie when the instrument panel short-circuited – it was changed in a record three minutes. Unfortunately, electrical problems persisted until the car was retired at 2.35am.

Jaguar XJR-9, No.1. Group C1. Entered by Tom Walkinshaw Racing and driven by Lammers/Scott/Tambay. This Jaguar was placed fourth on distance after completing 3195.90 miles at an average speed of 133.34mph. In spite of problems with the exhaust, a gearbox which had to be replaced at 6.15am and Tambay's bumper-to-bumper shunt at Tertre Rouge, this brilliant Jaguar took the lead on the 153rd lap and held it for five hours.

Jaguar XJR-9, No.2. Group C1. Entered by Tom Walkinshaw Racing and driven by Nielsen/Wallace/Cobb.
A host of minor problems plagued this car; at around 6.50pm there were problems with the shock absorbers, then at 9.04pm the bonnet had to be changed. At 10.55pm, Cobb left the road at Tertre Rouge and got stuck in the gravel before setting off again. At 5.18am the car passed Arnage in a cloud of smoke and returned to the pits to retire with a blown gasket. It was clocked at 241mph on the Mulsanne Straight.

Jaguar XJR-9, No.3. C1 Group. Entered by Tom Walkinshaw Racing and driven by Jones/Kline/Daly.
This car stopped at 6.58pm on the Mulsanne Straight with engine trouble – a valve had failed – and retired officially at 10.23pm.

Jaguar XJR-9, No.4. C1 category. Entered by Tom Walkinshaw Racing and driven by A. Ferté/M. Ferté/Salazar.
This Jaguar was placed eighth on distance after completing 3094.97 miles in 24 hours at an average speed of 129.07mph and was another car to be plagued with a series of mechanical problems and mishaps. Alain Ferté started the driving and stopped only eight minutes later to change a wheel. At 8.11pm the exhaust manifold was changed and at 4.18am the gearbox. Michel Ferté had a bumper-to-bumper shunt at the Ford bend at 5.52am and this was followed by more trouble with the exhaust at 6.44am. Another bumper-to-bumper took place at 8am. However, this Jaguar was clocked at 240mph and after falling from fifth to fifteenth place, seventeen laps behind the leaders, it climbed back to a very creditable eighth.

1990

During the close season, M. Balestre and the ACO engaged in a scuffle. As a result of this, chicanes appeared on the Mulsanne Straight to add 20 secs to lap times and the 1990 race temporarily lost World Championship status. Mercedes decided against entry, but may have regretted their decision as Jaguar, Porsche, Nissan, Toyota and Mazda fought a pitched battle of absorbing interest. Jaguar achieved 1–2 after the dramatic last-minute retirement while in second place of the heroically-driven Brun Motorsport Porsche. Spectator Sir John Egan left Jaguar on the crest of the wave created by his leadership.

Jaguar XJR12, No.1 Chassis No.990. Group C1. Entered by Silk Cut Jaguar/Tom Walkinshaw Racing Ltd and driven by Brundle/A Ferté/Leslie.

Retired in the 16th hour with water pump failure. From the beginning of the evening associated problems had disturbed its progress. Its retirement allowed Martin Brundle to join the crew of Jaguar No.3. But did they really need him?

Jaguar XJR12, No.2. Chassis No.290. Group C1. Entered by Silk Cut Jaguar/Tom Walkinshaw Racing Ltd and driven by Lammers/Wallace/Konrad.

This car finished second, 4 laps behind the winner, having covered 2998.19 miles at 125.29mph. Badly placed on the starting grid (9th row), No.2 was in third place within a quarter of an hour of the finish. Then, the luck of the Brun Motorsport Porsche No.16 in second place vanished, and brought joy to the drivers and mechanics of No.2, which thus assumed the mantle of runner-up.

Jaguar XJR12, No.3 Chassis No.1090. Group C1. Entered by Silk Cut Jaguar/Tom Walkinshaw Racing Ltd and driven by Nielsen/Cobb/Salazar (with help from Brundle). Finished first overall on distance, having completed 3032 miles at an average of 126.70mph. This Jaguar was timed at 219.83mph on the approach to the Nissan Chicane on what was now referred to as the 'late' Mulsanne Straight.

Despite these impressive speeds, the Jaguars began the race wisely, holding station behind Nissan and Porsche. During the evening, the pace increased and a savage struggle followed relative calm.

This car ran a superb race, and the team of No.3 only experienced a single minor braking problem during the entire event.

Jaguar XJR12, No.4 Chassis No.190. Group C1. Entered by Silk Cut Jaguar/Tom Walkinshaw Racing Ltd and driven by Jones/Perez Sala/M Ferté.
Retired in the 20th hour. This, the fastest TWR Jaguar in practice (7th overall), suffered engine failure only four hours from the finish.

1923 1989

The following tables indicate the principal characteristics of the marques covered in this Book: AC, Aston Martin, Austin-Healey, Bentley, Jaguar, Lotus, MG and Triumph. Each table shows the year, the race number of each car, the marque, type of engine (number of cylinders), engine capacity with supercharger or turbocharger where applicable and the weight.

YEAR	No.	MARQUE	ENGINE	CAP.(cc)	WEIGHT (in lbs)
1923	8	Bentley	4	2997	
1924	8	Bentley	4	2997	
1925	9	Bentley	4	3276	
	10	Bentley	4	3276	
1926	7	Bentley	4	2997	
	8	Bentley	4	2997	
	9	Bentley	4	2997	
1927	1	Bentley	4	4379	
	2	Bentley	4	2997	
	3	Bentley	4	2989	
1928	25	Aston Martin	4	1492	
	26	Aston Martin	4	1492	
	2	Bentley	4	4392	
	3	Bentley	4	4392	
	4	Bentley	4	4392	
1929	1	Bentley	6	6597	5500
	8	Bentley	4	4398	
	9	Bentley	4	4398	
	10	Bentley	4	4398	
	11	Bentley	4	4398	
1930	2	Bentley	6	6597	5500
	3	Bentley	6	6597	5500
	4	Bentley	6	6597	5500
	8	Bentley	4	4389(S)	
	9	Bentley	4	4389(S)	
	28	MG	4	847	
	29	MG	4	847	
1931	24	Aston Martin	4	1495	
	25	Aston Martin	4	1495	
	26	Aston Martin	4	1495	
	7	Bentley	4	4398	
	31	MG	4	747	
	32	MG	4	747	
1932	20	Aston Martin	4	1495	
	21	Aston Martin	4	1495	
	22	Aston Martin	4	1495	
	5	Bentley	4	4398(S)	
	32	MG	4	747	
1933	24	Aston Martin	4	1495	
	25	Aston Martin	4	1495	
	26	Aston Martin	4	1495	
	5	Bentley	4	4395(S)	
	38	MG	4	747(S)	
	41	MG	4	747(S)	

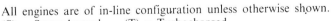

All engines are of in-line configuration unless otherwise shown.
(S) = Supercharged   (T) = Turbocharged

Bentley No.8, winner of the 1924 Le Mans 24 Hour Race.

YEAR	No.	MARQUE	ENGINE	CAP.(cc)	WEIGHT (in lbs)
1934	20	Aston Martin	4	1495	
	21	Aston Martin	4	1495	
	22	Aston Martin	4	1495	
	23	Aston Martin	4	1495	
	24	Aston Martin	4	1495	
	33	MG	6	1087(S)	
	34	MG	6	1087(S)	
	52	MG	4	847	
	53	MG	4	747	
1935	27	Aston Martin	4	1495	
	28	Aston Martin	4	1495	
	29	Aston Martin	4	1495	
	30	Aston Martin	4	1495	
	31	Aston Martin	4	1495	
	32	Aston Martin	4	1495	
	33	Aston Martin	4	1495	
	39	MG	6	1087	
	41	MG	6	1087	
	42	MG	6	1087	
	55	MG	4	847	
	56	MG	4	847	
	57	MG	4	847	
	58	MG	4	847(S)	
1937	31	Aston Martin	4	1942	
	32	Aston Martin	4	1974	
	37	Aston Martin	4	1495	
	54	MG	4	936	
1938	27	Aston Martin	4	1967	
	49	MG	4	954	
	50	MG	4	936	
1939	29	Aston Martin	4	1967	
	31	Aston Martin	4	1495	
	36	MG	4	847	
	47	MG	4	954	
1949	19	Aston Martin	6	2580	2860
	27	Aston Martin	4	1970	
	28	Aston Martin	4	1970	
	29	Aston Martin	4	1970	
	30	Aston Martin	4	1970	
	31	Aston Martin	4	1950	
	20	Healey	4	2443	
	6	Bentley	6	4246	
	43	MG	4	1250	
1950	19	Aston Martin	6	2581	2761
	20	Aston Martin	6	2581	
	21	Aston Martin	6	2581	
	14	Healey	6	3846	
	23	Healey	6	2443	
	11	Bentley	6	4252	
	12	Bentley	6	4252	
	15	Jaguar	6	3441	
	16	Jaguar	6	3441	
	17	Jaguar	6	3441	
	39	MG	4	1244	

YEAR	No.	MARQUE	ENGINE	CAP.(cc)	WEIGHT (in lbs)
1951	24	Aston Martin	6	2581	
	25	Aston Martin	6	2581	
	26	Aston Martin	6	2581	
	27	Aston Martin	6	2581	
	28	Aston Martin	6	2581	
	19	Healey	6	3846	
	14	Bentley	6	4252	
	20	Jaguar	6	3441	
	21	Jaguar	6	3441	
	22	Jaguar	6	3441	
	23	Jaguar	6	3441	
	43	MG	4	1250	
1952	25	Aston Martin	6	2581	
	26	Aston Martin	6	2581	
	27	Aston Martin	6	2581	
	31	Aston Martin	6	2581	
	32	Aston Martin	6	2581	
	17	Jaguar	6	3474	
	18	Jaguar	6	3474	
	19	Jaguar	6	3474	
1953	25	Aston Martin	6	2921	
	26	Aston Martin	6	2921	
	27	Aston Martin	6	2921	
	69	Aston Martin	6	2580	
	33	Austin-Healey	4	2663	
	34	Austin-Healey	4	2663	
	17	Jaguar	6	3442	
	18	Jaguar	6	3442	
	19	Jaguar	6	3442	
	20	Jaguar	6	3442	
1954	8	Aston Martin	6	4090(S)	2310
	20	Aston Martin	6	2921	
	21	Aston Martin	6	2921	
	22	Aston Martin	6	2921	
	27	Aston Martin	6	2921	2640
	12	Jaguar D	6	3441	2200
	14	Jaguar D	6	3441	
	15	Jaguar D	6	3441	
	16	Jaguar C	6	3441	
	62	Triumph TR2	4	1991	2013
1955	23	Aston Martin	6	2922	
	24	Aston Martin	6	2922	
	25	Aston Martin	6	2922	
	26	Austin-Healey	4	2662	
	6	Jaguar D	6	3442	
	7	Jaguar D	6	3442	
	8	Jaguar D	6	3442	
	9	Jaguar D	6	3442	
	10	Jaguar D	6	3442	
	48	Lotus IX	4	1097	
	41	MG EX182	4	1489	
	42	MG EX182	4	1489	
	64	MG EX182	4	1489	
	28	Triumph TR2	4	1991	
	29	Triumph TR2	4	1991	
	68	Triumph TR2	4	1991	

YEAR	No.	MARQUE	ENGINE	CAP.(cc)	WEIGHT (in lbs)
1956	8	Aston Martin	6	2922	
	9	Aston Martin	6	2922	
	14	Aston Martin	6	2493	
	1	Jaguar D	6	3441	
	2	Jaguar D	6	3441	2184
	3	Jaguar D	6	3441	2202
	4	Jaguar D	6	3441	
	5	Jaguar D	6	3441	
	6	Jaguar XK140	6	3441	
	32	Lotus XI	4	1459	
	35	Lotus XI	4	1098	
	36	Lotus XI	4	1098	
1957	31	AC Ace	6	1971	1872
	5	Aston Martin	6	3669	
	19	Aston Martin	6	2922	1958
	20	Aston Martin	6	2922	1892
	21	Aston Martin	6	2922	2235
	3	Jaguar D	6	3780	
	4	Jaguar D	6	3780	
	15	Jaguar D	6	3432	
	16	Jaguar D	6	3442	2312
	17	Jaguar D	6	3442	2131
	41	Lotus XI	4	1098	1045
	42	Lotus XI	4	1098	1056
	55	Lotus XI	4	744	946
	62	Lotus XI	4	1098	1060
1958	27	AC Ace	6	1970	1773
	28	AC LM	6	1970	1621
	2	Aston Martin	6	2921	2017
	3	Aston Martin	6	2921	1960
	4	Aston Martin	6	2921	2021
	5	Aston Martin	6	2992	2145
	6	Jaguar D	6	2987	2277
	7	Jaguar D	6	2987	2204
	8	Jaguar D	6	2987	2184
	9	Lister-Jaguar	6	2987	2136
	10	Lister-Jaguar	6	2987	2019
	11	Jaguar D	6	2987	2208
	57	Jaguar D	6	2987	2158
	26	Lotus XV	4	1965	1198
	35	Lotus XV	4	1476	1223
	38	Lotus XI	4	1098	1053
	39	Lotus XI	4	1098	1042
	55	Lotus XI	4	741	915
	56	Lotus XI	4	741	882
1959	29	AC Ace	6	1971	1788
	4	Aston Martin	6	2992	1883
	5	Aston Martin	6	2992	1892
	6	Aston Martin	6	2992	1900
	7	Aston Martin	6	2992	1843
	21	Aston Martin	6	2992	2789
	1	Lister-Jaguar	6	2996	2026
	2	Lister-Jaguar	6	2996	2015
	3	Jaguar D	6	2996	2050
	30	Lotus XV	4	1963	1276
	38	Lotus Elite	4	1221	1370

YEAR	No.	MARQUE	ENGINE	CAP.(cc)	WEIGHT (in lbs)
1959	41	Lotus Elite	4	1221	1375
	42	Lotus Elite	4	1221	1430
	53	Lotus XVII	4	742	860
	54	Lotus XVII	4	742	851
	33	MGA	4	1581	1922
	25	Triumph TR3	4	1985	2191
	26	Triumph TR3	4	1985	2125
	27	Triumph TR3	4	1985	2142
1960	30	AC	6	1971	1949
	57	AC	6	1971	1876
	7	Aston Martin	6	2992	1920
	8	Aston Martin	6	2992	
	23	Austin-Healey	6	2912	2618
	46	Austin-Healey	4	996	1256
	5	Jaguar	6	2997	
	6	Jaguar	6	2997	2046
	31	Lotus LX	4	1964	1566
	41	Lotus Elite	4	1216	
	42	Lotus Elite	4	1216	
	43	Lotus Elite	4	1216	1447
	44	Lotus Elite	4	1216	1425
	62	Lotus Elite	4	1216	1401
	32	MG	4	1762	1779
	28	Triumph	4	1985	2202
	29	Triumph	4	1985	
	59	Triumph	4	1985	
1961	28	AC	6	1971	1738
	29	AC	6	1991	1971
	1	Aston Martin	6	3670	2565
	2	Aston Martin	6	3670	2483
	3	Aston Martin	6	3670	2481
	4	Aston Martin	6	2992	1854
	5	Aston Martin	6	2992	1878
	21	Austin-Healey	6	2912	2354
	42	Austin-Healey	4	994	
	46	Austin-Healey	4	994	
	61	Austin-Healey	6	2912	2387
	38	Lotus Elite	4	1216	
	39	Lotus Elite	4	1216	
	40	Lotus Elite	4	1216	
	41	Lotus Elite	4	1216	1452
	51	Lotus Elite	4	742	
	62	Lotus Elite	4	1216	1386
	58	MGA	4	1762	1991
	25	Triumph TR4 S	4	1985	2134
	26	Triumph TR4 S	4	1985	
	27	Triumph TR4 S	4	1985	
1962	60	AC Ace	6	1971	1751
	11	Aston Martin	6	3996	2310
	12	Aston Martin	6	3749	2345
	14	Aston Martin	6	3749	2486
	24	Austin-Healey	6	2912	
	8	Jaguar E	6	3781	2629
	9	Jaguar E	6	3781	
	10	Jaguar E	6	3781	2459
	44	Lotus Elite	4	1216	1324

YEAR	No.	MARQUE	ENGINE	CAP.(cc)	WEIGHT (in lbs)
1962	45	Lotus Elite	4	1216	1326
	47	Lotus XXIII	4	997	1009
	48	Lotus XXIII	4	742	959
1963	7	Aston Martin	6	3749	2429
	8	Aston Martin	6	3749	2200
	18	Aston Martin	6	3995	2479
	19	Aston Martin	6	3749	2580
	42	Austin-Healey	4	1100	1480
	14	Jaguar E	6	3781	2433
	15	Jaguar E	6	3781	2462
	16	Jaguar E	6	3781	2422
	17	Lister Jaguar	6	3781	2431
	38	Lotus Elite	4	1216	1386
	39	Lotus Elite	4	1216	
	31	MGB	4	1803	1892
1964	18	Aston Martin	6	3751	2448
	53	Austin-Healey	4	1101	1452
	16	Jaguar E	6	3781	2574
	17	Jaguar E	6	3781	2514
	38	Lotus Elan	4	1593	1494
	43	Lotus Elite	4	1216	1511
	37	MGB	4	1891	2101
	49	Triumph Spit.	4	1147	1636
	50	Triumph Spit.	4	1147	1632
	65	Triumph Spit.	4	1147	1621
1965	48	Austin-Healey	4	1293	1531
	49	Austin-Healey	4	1293	1540
	39	MGB	4	1801	2076
	52	Triumph Spit.	4	1147	1518
	53	Triumph Spit.	4	1147	1531
	54	Triumph Spit.	4	1147	1511
	60	Triumph Spit.	4	1147	
1966	48	Austin-Healey	4	1293	1586
	49	Austin-Healey	4	1293	1584
1967	51	Austin-Healey	4	1293	1573
	44	Lotus Europa	4	1588	1353
1968	50	Austin Healey	4	1293	1474

YEAR	No.	MARQUE	ENGINE	CAP.(cc)	WEIGHT (in lbs)
1968	47	Healey	4	1968	1859
1969	37	Healey	4	1998	2024
1970	34	Healey	V8	2995	1959
1977	83	Aston Martin	V8	5340	3334
1979	50	Aston Martin	V8	5340(T)	
1982	31	Aston Martin	V8	5340	2303
	32	Aston Martin	V8	5340	2312
1983	39	Nimrod AM	V8	5340	1760
	41	Emka AM	V8	5340	
1984	31	Nimrod AM	V8	5340(T)	2156
	32	Nimrod AM	V8	5340(T)	
	40	Jaguar	V12	5945	2090
	44	Jaguar	V12	5945	
1985	40	Jaguar	V12	5945	2193
	44	Jaguar	V12	5945	2226
	24	Cheetah AM	V8	5340	2008
	66	Emka AM	V8	5340	
1986	51	Jaguar	V12	5993	1916
	52	Jaguar	V12	5993	1911
	53	Jaguar	V12	5993	1907
1987	4	Jaguar	V12	6900	1971
	5	Jaguar	V12	6900	1919
	6	Jaguar	V12	6900	1980
1988	1	Jaguar	V12	7000	1971
	2	Jaguar	V12	7000	1966
	3	Jaguar	V12	7000	2008
	21	Jaguar	V12	7000	2017
	22	Jaguar	V12	7000	2010
1989	1	Jaguar	V12	7000	2032
	2	Jaguar	V12	7000	2030
	3	Jaguar	V12	7000	2107
	4	Jaguar	V12	7000	2046
	18	Aston Martin	V8	6000	2162
	19	Aston Martin	V8	6000	2162
1990	1	Jaguar	V12	7000	2048
1990	2	Jaguar	V12	7000	2064
1990	3	Jaguar	V12	7000	2097
1990	4	Jaguar	V12	7000	2088

Acknowledgements

No book is written without a certain amount of outside help and encouragement.
My thanks to Peter Richley who unearthed in England the last few photographs that I needed.
To Monique Bouleux and Sylvie Chaudemanche, the indefatigable ladies of the Automobile Club de L'Ouest Press Relations department.
To Christian Moity for his knowledge of the 24 Hour Race and for his books written alone and in conjunction with Jean-Marc Teissedre.
To Madame Kerner-Villers, Bernard Salvat and Alain and Josy Redon for proof-reading.
To all the photographers who have lent me their pictures: Jean Fondin, Maurice-Louis Rosenthal, Philippe Dueux, Jean-Michel Dubois, Jean-François Galeron, Geoffrey Goddard, Studio Lafay, H. Beroul, Agence Autopress, LAT, and Quadrant Pictures Library.